Max Carocci

SHAMANS

THE VISUAL CULTURE OF ANIMISM,
HEALING & JOURNEYS TO OTHER PLANES

CONTENTS

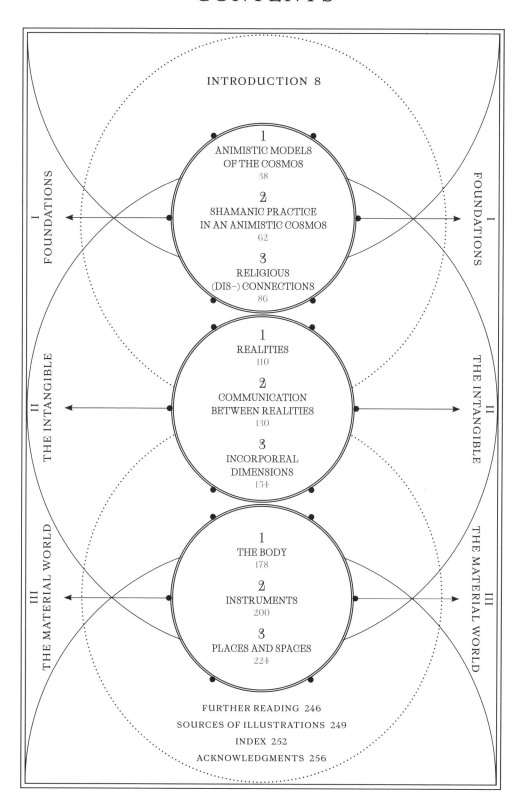

INTRODUCTION 8

I FOUNDATIONS

1 ANIMISTIC MODELS OF THE COSMOS 38

2 SHAMANIC PRACTICE IN AN ANIMISTIC COSMOS 62

3 RELIGIOUS (DIS-)CONNECTIONS 86

II THE INTANGIBLE

1 REALITIES 110

2 COMMUNICATION BETWEEN REALITIES 130

3 INCORPOREAL DIMENSIONS 154

III THE MATERIAL WORLD

1 THE BODY 178

2 INSTRUMENTS 200

3 PLACES AND SPACES 224

FURTHER READING 246
SOURCES OF ILLUSTRATIONS 249
INDEX 252
ACKNOWLEDGMENTS 256

INTRODUCTION

'There are some who are worshipped by the ignorant masses as though they were prophets, since, whenever questioned, they will give many predictions to many folk through the medium of a foul spirit which they call gand, and these auguries come true.'

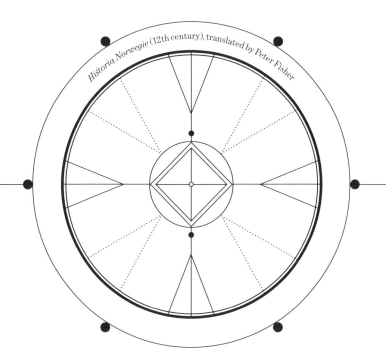

Historia Norwegie (12th century), translated by Peter Fisher

For centuries, the shaman has been a marginal figure at the crossroads between exoticism and contempt. Whether shunned by conventional faiths or admired as the embodiment of values antithetical to modernity, the shaman has been represented as an ambivalent mystical character that shares many traits with witches, exorcists and healers. The history of the term is riddled with ambiguities, but the art that shamans have produced offers a window into their animistic worlds and beliefs that challenge scientific worldviews and religious dogmas.

In 2023, the world-famous artist Marina Abramović (1946–) presented a site-specific installation at the Pitt Rivers Museum of Anthropology in Oxford, UK. Engaging with artefacts from the collection, she described how she worked with their essence and powers around the concept of 'presence in absence'. Abramović's longstanding interest in cross-cultural approaches to the immaterial led her to select objects associated with magic, initiation rites and transformative states of consciousness – all recurring themes in her artistic production. Though Abramović has researched shamanism and the anthropology of religion, she would not call herself a shaman. Nevertheless, the term 'shaman' has been applied to her and her work many times.

Abramović is not the only artist to be described thus. Art historians and popular commentators have associated shamanism with the lives and work of Jackson Pollock, Joseph Beuys, Paul Cézanne, Constantin Brâncuși, Wassily Kandinsky, Nam June Paik and many others. More recent artists deliberately reference shamanism in a variety of guises. Zadie Xa (1983–) bases her work on Korean shamanism and folklore. Canadian artist AA Bronson (1946–) is inspired by Native North American spiritualities, and the intentionally provocative performances of the British artist Marcus Coates (1968–) are based on tropes and ideas associated with shamanism.

Artists who demonstrate a relationship to the spiritual, the numinous, the mythological or the divine are frequently called shamans or shamanistic. Not coincidentally, the specialized literature in history of religion and anthropology describes shamans as individuals endowed with great creativity: liminal figures with a deep connection to what we conventionally call the 'supernatural'. Some find the classification of contemporary artists as shamans convincing. Most scholars, however, criticize it as a form of exoticism, or misinformed romanticism, that broadens the term's meaning so much as to render it virtually useless. That the

‹ *page 8*
Christoph von Fürer-Haimendorf, Apatani shaman, 1945
The Apatani are one of the many Indigenous groups of the Himalayan region, where shamans still hold an important ritual role despite external influences.

Henning Christoph, Mongolian shaman curing a child, Khövsgöl, Mongolia

As part of a ceremony to cure an unwell child, the shaman chants, invoking invisible entities, while holding long, tubular fringes that represent snakes. Shamanism in Mongolia has experienced a vigorous comeback in the post-Soviet period.

Marcus Coates, *Journey to the Lower World (Coot)*, Liverpool, 2004
In this piece, Coates performed a self-designed ritual for residents of a tower block in Liverpool that was awaiting demolition.

same term can be so readily applied to both artists and ritual specialists indicates that the word 'shaman' means different things to different people, irrespective of their cultural, historical or geographical context.

There is a general consensus that Siberia and Central Asia are shamanism's homelands. Ancient images on boulders and rock shelters in the region show items that look similar to such shamanic accoutrements as feather headdresses, drums, fringed coats, mirrors, weapons and ritual batons. Since records began, shamans from these regions have been using these items. However, such connections between rock art and shamanic practice may be conjectural, and rock art is notoriously difficult to date.

Central Asian and Siberian shamanisms feature some of the most elaborate versions of animistic beliefs, and these beliefs go back a very long way; the linguistic roots underpinning variations of the word 'shaman' are extremely ancient. Key concepts include: a tiered, animated and sentient cosmos;

George Catlin, *Medicine Man, Performing His Mysteries Over a Dying Man*, 1832
Scholars do not agree as to whether the healing practices of certain North American peoples can be considered shamanic.

Huichol shaman heals a patient, San Luis Potosí, Mexico, 2000
Shamanism is integral to the Huichol's cultural survival because it encapsulates their beliefs and values.

the permeability of reality's visible and invisible dimensions; the transference of invisible powers between beings; the existence and agency of other-than-human entities; bodily transformations; the belief in a free soul that can undertake transcendental travels; and the reality of visions and dreams.

Scholarly opinion is divided over the geographical spread of shamanism, and the presence (or absence) of the phenomenon of the spirit journey managed by the shaman is usually a defining feature of this debate. Places where trance takes the form of spirit possession – as in large parts of Africa, Oceania and Europe – are mostly excluded from the discourse of shamanism; yet the Americas, where practitioners are in full charge of their metaphysical journeys, may be included. Arguably, not all individuals in dissociative states may be considered shamans, even if they enter what is known as an 'Alternative (or Adjusted) State of Consciousness' (ASC) to communicate with the intangible, because shamans' trances aim specifically

Robber's Roost, also known as Shaman's Cave, Arizona
Whether this cave has ever been used by shamans or not, its name shows the popular appeal of shamanism among New Age practitioners.

to cure, heal or intercede with intangible forces on behalf of the community. Shamans are also herbalists, guides to the dead (or psychopomps), counsellors, community protectors and spiritual leaders – functions that, in most cultures, are not necessarily covered by a single person who goes into a trance. Classic distinctions between shamanic and non-shamanic cultures are thus based on shamans' responsibilities towards their respective societies, and the place they hold in the group's social organization.

As noted above, the word 'shaman' has ancient roots. Experts locate its linguistic origins in a Tungusic/Siberian source (*šaman*, referring to a person who is in a state of enraptured excitement), though a minority of scholars link it to a term from Sanskrit/Indo-European languages spoken further south (*śramaṇa*, an ascetic or mystic). Regardless of its origins, the term has been freely applied in its modern spelling 'shaman' to various spiritual practitioners in wildly differing contexts, ranging from Indigenous peoples of South America to European Neo-Pagans, and from East African possession cults to New Agers from Sedona, Arizona.

Theodor de Bry, after Jacques Le Moyne de Morgues, 'Outina, going at the Head of his Army, Consults a Sorcerer', from Volume 2 (1591) of *America* Descriptions of Timucua diviners suggest that the state of rapture illustrated here may be part of a shamanic ritual.

Written descriptions of shamanic practices date as far back as the ancient Greek historian Herodotus (*c.* fifth century BCE), in his account of the Scythians. The *Historia Norwegie* ('History of Norway') of *c.* 1160 CE described such practices among medieval Scandinavian Saami. The term 'shaman' itself, however, was first used during the Enlightenment. Two of the earliest eyewitnesses, the Orthodox Archpriest Avvakum Petrov (1620–1682) and the Dutch traveller Nicolaes Witsen (1641–1717), used the local term 'shaman' to describe practitioners among the Siberian peoples they visited who willingly went into a trance. 'Shaman' and 'shamanism' were eventually adopted in descriptions of Native American ritual specialists through the work of anthropologists Roland Dixon (1875–1934) and John Reed Swanton (1873–1958).

As interest in shamanism grew over the years, it became associated with a host of ritual practitioners who employed ASCs, including the Egyptian and Sudanese Zār cult exorcists described

PROFILE
SHAMANS IN ANTIQUITY

New theories are helping contemporary archaeologists to build ever more complex pictures of past societies. Old interpretations based on iconographic and ethnographic analysis are giving way to sophisticated reconstructions and contextualizations. Though shamanism's historical depth and geographical spread are still debated, new frameworks engender more reliable perspectives on prehistoric religious ideologies, including various forms of shamanism. The 2000–1750 BCE Okunev stele below, from southern Siberia, depicts a sun spirit who may have assisted shamans.

STAG SKULL HEADDRESS
Horned headdresses have been almost universally associated with shamans. Specimens from several archaeological sites point to widespread ceremonialism related to deer, and reindeer are especially important in Eurasian shamanic groups. Claims about the antiquity of shamanism have often been based on this headdress (*c*. 8000 BCE) found at Star Carr, UK, and similar finds.

SORCERER CAVE PAINTING
This is a reproduction of a painting in the Cave of the Trois-Frères in Ariège, France, which is thought to date from *c*. 13,000 BCE. This puzzling part-human, part-animal hybrid figure, named the Sorcerer, has been interpreted as one of the earliest images of a shaman. At present, it is impossible to determine the meaning of the painting.

SHIGIR IDOL
Thought to be the oldest carved wooden statue in the world at around 12,500 years old, this long anthropomorphic pole, found in a peat bog in Russia's Ural mountains, is used as evidence of the antiquity of shamanism. Its rib cage and humanoid face are thematically similar to modern examples from Asia and the American Arctic and so may suggest a shamanic character.

HARPOON COUNTERWEIGHT
Objects employed across the Alaskan Bering Strait as spear-throwing weights, such as this example (300–500 CE), might have used their winged shape to confer a bird's power of flight to darts. Eye-like designs on some may indicate the ability to see. Using an object's inherent power points to a history of shamanic thinking in the American Arctic.

FISH-MAN SCULPTURE
This *c*. 10,000–7000 BCE carving from the Lepenski Vir site in Serbia displays human and fish attributes, notably including human arms and hands, and a fish-like mouth. This and similar examples from the same archaeological culture point to ideas of shape-shifting and transformation, indicating, for some people, a possible instance of prehistoric shamanic thinking.

PORTRAIT OF A WOMAN
The individuality of the face carved into this mammoth tusk 26,000 years ago prompts some to call it a portrait. It was uncovered at Dolní Věstonice in the Czech Republic. Burials that display unusual accoutrements and paraphernalia are often interpreted as belonging to ritual specialists, who some claim to be shamans. At present there is no way of telling these roles apart.

DECODING PASHUPATI SEAL

Those trying to prove the antiquity of shamanism have used evidence from different backgrounds and regions. A particular object named the Pashupati seal (c. 2700–2100 BCE) from the prehistoric culture of Pakistan's Indus Valley displays ambiguous imagery that most see as an early representation of the god Shiva, but may also be interpreted in light of what is known of shamanism today. Unfortunately, the script on Indus Valley seals has not yet been deciphered, so current readings are merely based on iconographic analysis.

1.

2.

3.

HORNS OR ANTLERS
The figure's headdress, made from horn or antlers, is analogous to the typical shamanic headdress employed by practitioners in many parts of Asia. Paired with other elements in the composition, this may suggest a shaman-like figure.

OTHER-THAN-HUMAN BEINGS
Though not identifiable in this seal, hybrid animals appear in many seals from this culture. They may be composite beings that have no correspondence in this reality. Their otherworldly character may indicate that they belong to a shamanic cosmology.

TRIPARTITE FACE
Common in visual representations of the god Shiva, the tripartite face visible here may also be a metaphor for someone who can see in all directions. The three faces could also be a shaman alongside two of his spirit helpers.

4.

5.

6.

TIGER
Powerful animals often accompany shamans as their doubles, helpers or mediators. To the right of the figure on this seal is a tiger with visible claws. Tigers have a central role in Asian mythology and, in some parts of the continent, are shamans' helpers.

YOGA POSITION
Visual representations of shamans frequently show them seated. The seated yoga posture visible here may suggest the figure's deep state of concentration, though at present it is not known if yoga has ever been used in shamanic practice.

ERECT PHALLUS
One of Shiva's avatars (Lakulisha) is typically represented with an erect phallus, which is a metaphor for male energy. Shamans, too, are often depicted with exaggerated male genitals to highlight their sexual potency and spiritual power.

by anthropologist Ioan Lewis (1930–2014), or initiates of the Bwiti secret cults from Gabon who were glossed as 'shamans' by Lyle Steadman (1934–) and Craig Palmer (1957–). However, the frequent lack of ethnographic detail, and incomplete or imprecise information about trance, social roles and associated beliefs, in many accounts resulted in potentially inappropriate attributions of the term to individuals who practised only oracular or magical functions. These inaccuracies have prompted many scholars to suggest that the word 'shaman' should be applied only to Siberia and to advocate the use of local definitions for other regions. Here the term will be used to introduce a variety of practitioners that have historically been called 'shamans' in order to acknowledge the complex histories and debates that surround the term and its various applications.

As community protectors, shamans fight negative forces, or what some call 'black magic'. In animistic societies across the world, this work falls under the rubric of healing and cure, because ailments, illnesses and diseases are believed to have a spiritual, intangible origin that the shamans must tackle. Among the Inuit

'Indian witch doctor healing a sick woman', Northwest Coast of North America, late 19th century–early 20th century
The staged scene depicted in this postcard only marginally resembles a shaman's healing session. Objects visible in the background are useless props that serve to convey an idea of otherness. The healer is holding a bone, possibly in reference to carved bone tubes used to suck disease out of the patient's body. The colours are visibly artificial and do not correspond to the muted tones of Pacific Northwest Coast art.

Saami shaman's vision, from Samuel Rheen's *En kortt Relation om Lapparnes Lefwarne och Sedher, wijdskiepellsser, sampt i många Stycken Grofwe wildfarellsser* (1671) In this interpretation of a shaman's vision, a devilish figure towers over the reclined shaman, revealing minister Samuel Rheen's perception of Saami traditional practices.

and other Indigenous American peoples, the theft of a person's soul by an evil entity may be the cause of a physical illness, and the shaman must travel to the subterranean realms to retrieve the soul for the benefit of their patient. In places such as Korea or South East Asia, physical or mental ill health is thought to originate in the breaking of taboos, misinterpretation of ancestors' guidance or defiance of ritual proscriptions. In those regions, shamans confirm the cause of the illness by receiving messages from the worlds beyond the visible and reporting them back to the living.

Shamans fall on a continuum that connects magic, faith and healing. Their practice always straddles the fine line between empirical proof and belief. Yet it would be incorrect to call shamanism a religion, because shamans mostly operate outside any organized structure based on doctrines, liturgies and clerical hierarchies. Shamans may at times work alongside, or even within, these structures, as in ancient China and Korea, or the Mongolian empire. There, shamans held official positions within an organized clergy, but their role was reduced

PROFILE
EUROPEAN DEPICTIONS OF SHAMANS THROUGH HISTORY

Knowledge about shamans appears in early Islamic, Christian and Chinese texts, but it isn't until the context of the European Enlightenment in the late seventeenth and eighteenth centuries that a systematic discourse on shamanism first develops. Most representations of shamans produced by Europeans focused on idolatry, paganism and devil worship. In the 1692 illustration opposite, for example, Nicolaes Witsen labels this Siberian shaman 'Priest of the Devil' and depicts him with clawed feet. Later on, anthropology treated shamanism as a 'primitive' religion and Soviet historiography talked about it as 'false consciousness' that needed to be eradicated. Visual representations of shamans testify to the biases, misconceptions and romanticization projected by Europeans onto shamans and their cultures.

THE CONJUROR OR THE FLYER
The terms 'conjuror' and 'flyer' used to describe this Native American figure indicate his ability to connect with the intangible world. Depicted by John White in c. 1585–90, this may be one of the earliest representations of an Indigenous American shaman.

CALIFORNIAN SHAMAN COSTUME
This romanticized depiction of a shaman from Baja California, Mexico, was included in a book of international 'costumes' to appeal to European audiences curious about foreign peoples' clothing and customs. It was created by Jacques Grasset de Saint-Sauveur and L. F. Labrousse and published in 1796.

RUSSIAN FEMALE SHAMAN
This Buryat shaman from a book depicting the inhabitants of Russia reflects the European taste for the exotic that was popular in the early 19th century. While vaguely resembling the real clothing, the figures drawn by Jean-Baptiste Benoît Eyriès are mostly invented.

FINGO WITCH DOCTOR
Labelled 'witch doctors' by the artist Barbara Tyrrell, reflecting the language of the early 20th century, these African ritual specialists have been considered shamans by some. The realism of this 1948 image reflects a search for authenticity and objectivity that was typical of ethnography in the 20th century.

Shaman in a trance, Ladakh, 2008 *Himalayan shamans may become vessels for the manifestations of gods and goddesses that speak through them while they are in a trance state. In Himalayan shamanism, the shaman's body becomes the temporary conduit of knowledge provided by invisible entities.*

to divination, weather forecasting or fortune-telling once they were integrated into the official state religion. In other contexts, priests may perform some 'shamanic' duties; for example, ingesting psychotropic agents to communicate with incorporeal entities that affect human life. There is evidence for this at the sites of Chavín de Huántar in Peru (1200–500 BCE) and Paquimé in Mexico (1200–1300 CE).

The issues of classification and nomenclature at the core of debates on shamanism remain unresolved. Disputes continue to revolve around whether to call ancient Norse seers shamans or diviners; whether South Africa's *sangomas* are shamans or just healers; or if individuals in various states of possession can be understood through shamanic models. There are sharply differing views about when a ritual practitioner may or may not be called a shaman. For example, whether to include among shamans all those that adopt ASCs to communicate with intangible entities – be they ancestors, spirits, non-material beings or incorporeal forms of existing people. Clearly, shamanism is neither a homogeneous nor an objective category. As a consequence, we are faced with multiple uses of a very charged term and a plurality of ever-evolving shamanisms that continue to emerge in different parts of the world.

An article published in 2022 stated that shamanism, in the broadest definition of the term, is the fastest growing 'religion' in England and Wales. This trend is mirrored in nations such as Hungary, Finland and Russia, where different forms of shamanism have recently emerged or made a vigorous comeback. This phenomenon may be linked to issues of revitalization, cultural recovery or revival, alternative spiritualities, or disenchantment with modernity and new religious movements.

The modern fascination with shamanism most likely arises as a response to society's perceived inability to provide satisfactory answers to the existential and spiritual crises of the times, with the secularization of society that followed colonialism, industrialization and the rise of Communism in eastern countries.

 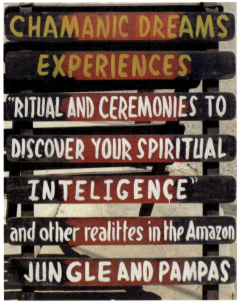

Georgiy Khoroshevskiy, Soviet propaganda poster, 'Elect workers to the Indigenous council. Don't let the shaman and the kulak in', 1931
The Soviet regime perceived shamans as enemies of the state because they promoted false consciousness through their belief in the supernatural.

Max Carocci, *Chamanic Dreams Experiences*, 2017
This board advertises shamanic rituals in the Bolivian Amazon, where shamanism contributes to tropical tourism.

Communist ideological emphasis on materialism and secularism forced shamans underground. They were punished for practising their arts and some were imprisoned. Training new apprentices became extremely difficult and oral traditions were forgotten. Ritual equipment, masks, drums and ceremonial implements were confiscated, burned, dispatched to rich collectors or sold to museums. However, in nations of the former Soviet Union, shamanism made a comeback after the collapse of the USSR in the early 1990s. Renewed confidence in the power of shamans emerged as a form of affirmation of community, or Indigenous identity, and shamanism was seen as a healthy counterpart to the hyper-industrialized, technologized and commercially driven worlds promoted in the new economic regimes established since the fall of the Eastern Bloc.

While in Russia and China shamanism remained dormant and almost forgotten for several decades, in remote regions of the Amazon, Malaysia and tribal India it retained links with the past, and yet continued to absorb different degrees of external influence, just as it had always done. Perceived to be closer to precolonial beliefs, these shamanisms may appear more authentic than the ones that were revived, or that emerged, in the twentieth century. Yet seeking the one original, 'authentic' shamanism is an impossible quest. There is no such thing. Cultures everywhere dynamically mutate over time through both internal dynamics and external inputs. These processes can be clearly traced during the second part of the twentieth century, when decolonization, the rise of countercultural movements, the decline of Russia's influence on its allies, and the liberalization of markets across the world resulted in shamanism's slow but steady comeback after years of virtual disappearance.

Around the middle of the twentieth century, partly driven by the publication of seminal texts by such scholars and intellectuals as R. Gordon Wasson, Mircea Eliade, Allen Ginsberg and Carlos Castaneda, popular curiosity about shamanism began as an interest in the mind-altering potential of psychotropic plants used by Indigenous healers. In 1960s North America, ideas and texts shared via countercultural networks prompted a record number of young

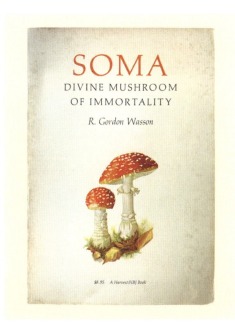

◁ Cover of R. Gordon Wasson's *Soma: Divine Mushroom of Immortality* (1972)
Wasson's experimentation with Mexican Mazatec healers produced many theories. For example, his books, including Soma, hypothesized that the sacred drink mentioned in the Rig Veda was derived from a hallucinogenic mushroom, making a connection between the shamanic use of mushrooms and sacred Hindu practices.

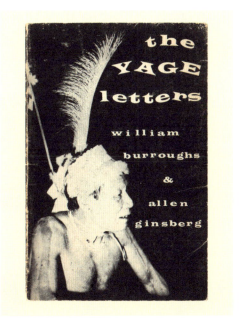

▷ Cover of William Burroughs and Allen Ginsberg's *The Yage Letters* (1963)
The correspondence between beat generation poet Allen Ginsberg and writer William Borroughs is one of the pivotal texts that exposed Western audiences to ayahuasca and shamanism.

people to travel to Mexico and South America to 'find themselves' and experiment with psychoactive substances. Such phenomena flourished as a result of disillusionment with the conformity promoted by cultures of consumerism and the ideologies of family and nation. Younger generations adopted lifestyles based on ecology, equality and freedom, while seeking alternative sources of spiritual enrichment not provided by structured faiths. Even today, this seems to be the main motivation to join shamanic groups, workshops or retreats.

During the twentieth century, liberal policies aimed at investing in cultural heritage around the world contributed to a rush to capitalize on Indigenous arts and traditions. This ultimately led to the marketing of local customs, including shamanism and its practitioners, who since the mid-twentieth century had turned the mounting rise of cultural tourism to their advantage. Economic liberalization encouraged both individuals and communities to promote shamanism in response to the West's increasing appetite for alternative spiritualities. Fuelled by the demand for shamanic-themed paraphernalia, new markets emerged for the production and sale of ceremonial instruments, remedies and fine art.

By 2000 spiritual tourism had reached astonishing proportions. Ecuador, Bolivia and Peru, but also the United States, Mexico, Siberia, Mongolia and other places, developed infrastructures and services aimed at thousands of visitors interested in shamanic worship and pilgrimage sites or in learning or experiencing shamanic knowledge and teachings. Critics describe such operations as cynical, callous enterprises that have little to do with the spirituality sought by tourists looking for a quick fix for their modern malaise.

Though often genuine in their intent, these initiatives have also been rejected by many Indigenous intellectuals and cultural gatekeepers as forms of neocolonialism. The appropriation of Indigenous knowledge by many self-styled shamans, the privilege inherent in the power to lay claim to other peoples' cultures, and the romanticization projected onto

Maxim Sukharev, *A Man with a Staff*, 2022

Russian artist Maxim Sukharev's imagery illustrates themes and motifs from ancient Slavic religion. This artwork makes reference to Slavic healers/priests called volkhv, *whose knowledge and wisdom has been associated with shamans. Shamanism has been revived in many Slavic-speaking countries today.*

Shamanic ritual from Simona Piantieri's documentary *Shamans and the City*, 2025
Western practitioners include shamanic drumming in their rituals to cure and heal.

Native peoples' beliefs and practices have been trenchantly criticized and labelled as abusive and disrespectful. In several Indigenous groups there are some people who see such activities as diametrically opposed to local shamanisms, which are usually perceived to be closer to their traditions than intrusive and denaturalizing elements imposed from the outside.

Couched in New Age spirituality, the forms of shamanism attacked by purists were comprehensively integrated into 'Core Shamanism', an approach to shamanic practice conceived by ex-anthropologist-turned healer Michael Harner (1929–2018). In his book *The Way of the Shaman* (1980), he reduced shamanism to a few basic principles, such as astral travel, drumming and healing, claiming that anyone with proper training could become a shaman by following a few easy steps. Core Shamanism stripped away all the inconvenient aspects of the practice, including risky battles against negative forces, and long years of apprenticeship.

Core Shamanism's edulcorated version of the practice, with its emphasis on healing, undoubtedly

Nicholas Roerich,
Sorcerers, 1905
These practitioners, called volkhvs, have been described as the predecessors of contemporary shamans active in the Slavic Native Faith.

resonated with the positive messages of self-discovery, universal spirituality and ecological regeneration spread by New Agers since the 1980s. Its syncretic, creative and individualistic nature is well suited to the multicultural dimension of the hectic and fragmented life of today, in which many individuals find themselves in need of self-care, belonging and transcendental meanings. A host of magazines, associations, social groups and websites exist for followers of Core Shamanism, who now probably outnumber those who follow older, traditional belief systems in which shamanism plays a part. Often collectively labelled 'Neo-Shamanism', these newer forms of spiritual practice are as different from one another as Peruvian Ayahuasca shamans, using crystals and Christian prayers, are from Scandinavian followers of pre-Christian religions, in which drumming and trance sessions are a central component.

Some forms of Neo-Shamanism are a syncretic mix of inspirations from a multiplicity of sources

that underpin political and nationalistic projects (not uncommonly linked to far-right extremism). Groups based on Celtic, German and Anglo-Saxon traditions that claim shamanism as part of their heritage emerged in the process of creating alternative spiritualities drawing on the perceived authenticity of the pre-industrial past. New religious movements, such as Neo-Paganism, Slavic Native Faith or Hungary's Turanism, integrated shamanism to signal their rejection of what they perceived to be the imposition of external worldviews over 'Indigenous' cosmologies and faiths.

Some have criticized these movements as artificial and contrived. Such processes, however, are ultimately no different from any other form of resistance underpinned by religious and spiritual meanings, and which hold up a pristine version of the past in contrast to a decadent and unappealing present. Many groups aim to re-establish links to what they see as unadulterated versions of history. Notable examples are Finnish, Estonian and Scandinavian Neo-Pagan groups, for whom shamanism is a powerful metaphor for social change and alternative lifestyles. Followers of the Old Norse religion and Finno-Ugrian animism claim to have direct and legitimate links to ancient shamanic customs and techniques. Aided by textual, archival and archaeological evidence, some Scandinavian Neo-Pagans are now interpreting historical figures, such as female seers (*völvas*) and male magicians (*seiðmaðr*), into shamans. Along with other narratives that support nativistic movements, this has contributed to the belief in shamanism as the 'first religion'. This notion, however, depends on a set of sweeping generalizations, superficial comparisons and universalizing pretences and has been very heavily criticized.

The many different positions adopted across time and space show a multifaceted, uneven and heterogeneous discourse. The cacophony of voices that compete for legitimacy in today's world make both the theory and the practice of shamanism a context in which extreme viewpoints variably align, or ultimately clash.

> *pages 34–35*
> Nanna Heitmann, Tuvan shamans, Yenisei River, Kyzyl, Russia, 2018
> *Male and female shamans at a fire ceremony in Tuva. Shamanic gatherings have gained popularity in the region since the collapse of the Soviet Union.*

Isogaisa Festival, Lavangen, Norway, 2015

This festival takes place in Saapmi (land of the Saami). The Saami were forced to renounce shamanism in the 17th century, but today the practice has seen a comeback. The increasing frequency of shamanic gatherings across the world is a symptom of the renewed interest in shamanism as a form of spiritual practice.

FOUNDATIONS

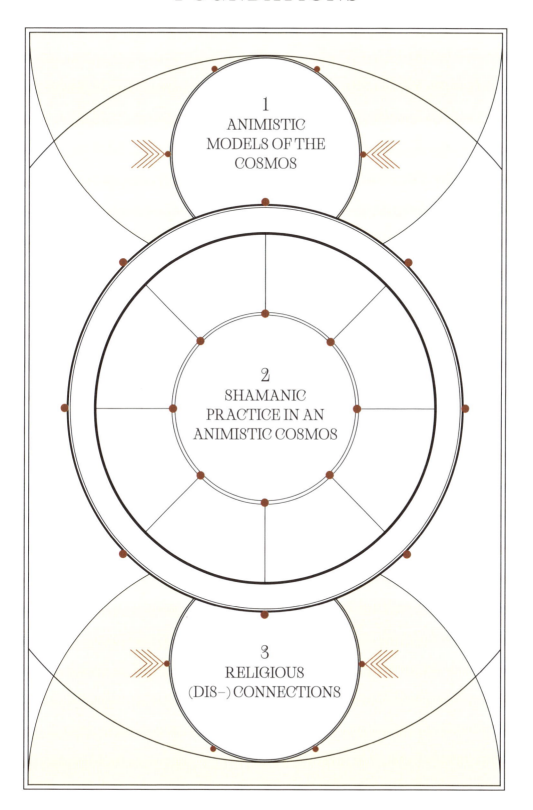

FOUNDATIONS

ANIMISTIC MODELS OF THE COSMOS

'Illness is like a person; it hears. Everything is alive; there is nothing dead in the world. The people say the dead are dead; but they are very much alive.'

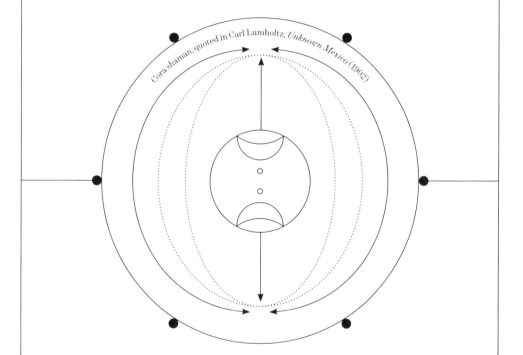

Cora shaman, quoted in Carl Lumholtz, *Unknown Mexico* (1902)

Shamans operate in realities structured along principles that do not follow scientific parameters. Their realities defy the laws of physics and admit as real experiences what some may call illusionary. Shamans confidently talk to animals and plants, cross tangible and intangible dimensions with ease, and send their souls to fight against their opponents. Species may adopt each other's point of view, often revealing their true essence as persons who act like humans do. From an animistic perspective, what appears to be illusion is the ultimate reality.

The daily practice of sprinkling milk in the four cardinal directions, Mongolians say, is part of an ancient custom. Many people still follow this tradition, and so do their shamans, who through this ritual gesture acknowledge their relationship with all the elements that populate their universe: the sky, rivers, rocks and mountains, but also the ancestors and the invisible powers that make the clouds move and water flow. The animated cosmos in which they operate is peopled by many entities able to act in, and affect, the world. This perspective is shared by hundreds of peoples across the world, for whom humans are only one among the universe's many inhabitants capable of action, choice and volition. Conventionally called animism, this approach to the living cosmos frequently depends on the presence of ritual specialists, whose role is to maintain the balance of forces that permeate both visible and invisible realms, cast away evil influences, and restore health among the members of their communities. Shamans take on this responsibility on behalf of their communities within the context of an animistic lifeworld.

The word 'animism' was popularized by the anthropologist Edward Burnett Tylor (1832–1917), who adopted it from Enlightenment thinkers, in his studies on the origins of belief published in *Primitive Religion* (1871). Tylor defined animism as the mistaken attribution of a soul to inanimate objects, which, he claimed, characterized the early stages of religious development. The term has Latin origins: *animus* is the Latin word for a soul or a spirit, and Tylor thought it a fitting description of this belief system. He maintained that animism was still detectable among so-called 'primitive' peoples that anthropologists were studying during his time. Both he and his contemporaries considered these peoples the remnants of a bygone era, their beliefs stuck in a perennial prehistoric stage from which they could not emancipate themselves. Tylor argued that, over the centuries, animism was gradually replaced by more elaborate, complex and refined religious forms, and was ultimately discredited by rational modern science.

< *page 36*
William Henry Jackson, Nanai shaman, Siberia, 1895
Although Siberian shamans share commonalities, there are variations in practice and tradition across different regions.

< *page 38*
Korean ink drawing
Korean shamans employ paintings such as this one to summon the characters pictured to aid them in their ceremonies. The gods, goddesses and deceased shamans depicted are manifested when ritually activated.

Milk libation, Mongolia, 2013 — *Offerings of mare's milk are common among Central Asian peoples. Horses are important shamanic animals that accompany the deceased in the afterlife and shamans on their spirit journeys. Offerings of vodka and melted butter are also common during festivals and communal rituals.*

Tlingit shaman's ivory amulet, *c.* 1870
A wide range of amulets, charms and pendants were used by Tlingit and other Pacific Northwest shamans. The meanings behind some of the imagery may be obscure to outside observers.

Tlingit shaman's bone pendant
Birds, mammals and other animals have an important role in Tlingit shamanic practice, and were used in healing sessions and ceremonies.

Many still talk about shamanism as the 'original religion', an idea elaborated from Tylor's theories. This notion suggests that ancient peoples shared an organized faith based around the figure of the shaman. Even in widespread forms of religion, however, there are considerable regional variations and different levels of complexity, and such divergences are not considered by Tylor's outdated model. There are fundamental differences, for example, in the ways shamanism is configured in hunting, agricultural or pastoral societies. Ideas about the soul and the relative importance of ancestors and deities may also distinguish the different forms of animism with which shamanism is frequently associated. The conflation of shamanism with animism is also erroneous because animism is not always necessarily associated with the role of the shaman.

What Tylor did not consider was that animistic perspectives reoccur in most world religions, and even in the contemporary Western societies with which he was familiar. Tylor was not ready to acknowledge the many instances in which religious believers of his time attributed life and agency to objects and inanimate things. Then as now, humans talk to statues, ask images for blessings, carry protective amulets or believe in relics' power of healing. All these examples could, and still can, be seen in the beliefs and practices common in various forms of organized religion, from Judaism to Islam, from Hinduism to Christianity,

< **Olmec transformation figurine, Mexico, 900–300 BCE**
Figurines of this kind have been interpreted as representing shape-shifting shamans, although the existence of shamanism among the Olmec has been questioned.

> **Olmec-style pendant, Mexico, 1000–500 BCE**
This pendant depicts a human head wearing a duck mask. Pre-Columbian peoples used masks to manifest gods and other intangible beings, a practice that is common across the Americas.

and even among atheists. Believers from each of these faiths may incorporate an animistic perspective into broader religious frameworks, but this does not constitute a separate faith.

Although people frequently talk of animism as if it were a form of religion, specialist scholars see it more as an attitude to the world of experience than an organized set of beliefs linked by shared liturgies, theology and beliefs. Though an animistic perspective may become the predominant, or even all-encompassing, model that makes sense of phenomenal and extra-sensory experiences, it may also be couched within more organized forms of belief, such as those ruled by proscriptions and prescriptions, guided by sacred texts and articulated in complex hierarchies of ritual specialists and attendants.

Given this evidence, today it would probably be more appropriate to talk of animism as a disposition towards experience, one that cuts across religious differences and that can appear in different configurations, for example in relation to the practice of shamanism. Not all societies that adopt a broadly animistic worldview employ shamans,

Waldemar Jochelson, Tungus shaman with drum, Siberia, 1901

The small anthropomorphic figurines on this shaman's apron are his personal invisible assistants that aid him on his spiritual travels. Coats, aprons, capes and tunics are shamans' personal armour, and represent and manifest the beings they rely on for help.

although shamans are intimately linked to animistic perspectives on the world.

There are other reasons why Tylor's definition is no longer applicable, and that is because it is heavily infused with Christian theology. In Tylor's time, the notion that an object may be mistakenly believed to have a soul seemed appropriate to make sense of the different ways in which artefacts, natural phenomena, animals and plants were variably attributed agency, intentionality and vitality. Yet, as most current scholars argue, the notion of the soul has deep Christian overtones and may not be directly translatable to or from the many languages spoken by peoples with an animistic worldview.

What is more, Tylor's definition relied on the Western distinction between the materiality of the body and the evanescence of spirit. This separation had significant implications for how Western thinkers treated what is real and tangible, and what is allegedly illusionary and incorporeal. This is a distinction that in animistic models does not apply. Corporeal and intangible registers of reality – from an animistic perspective – are fluid, porous and deeply intertwined. At times they may be interchangeable and overlapping. Bodies are fundamentally unstable, humans can shape-shift, animals may reveal their inner human nature, and what appears real to our eyes is often just an illusion.

This is why, among many animistic peoples, appearance is often less relevant than how a being behaves in the world of the living. It is a being or entity's actions that may give away its true essence, and this concept is abundantly depicted in the visual expressions from animistic regions. Artists from different traditions have adopted various strategies to convey this idea, as can be seen in the exploration of perspectivism overleaf.

Similarly inventive have been the visual solutions devised to convey the idea of a universe composed of multiple layers of reality, only some of which are accessible to humans in ordinary circumstances. This is what may be called a 'multiverse' to convey the overlapping, simultaneous existence of different

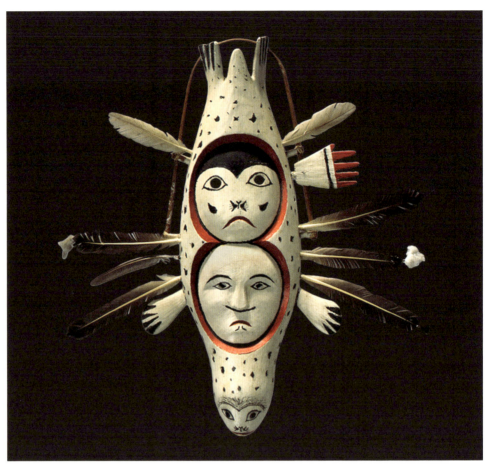

DECODING PERSPECTIVISM

The notion that species can adopt each other's point of view is depicted in multiple ways by Indigenous American peoples. This idea is called perspectivism, which implies the personhood of certain animal species. This can be expressed by revealing a human face under an animal's skin, as in the Yup'ik seal mask shown above, or showing an animal body with human features. Equally, humans can take on the guise of animals. Appearances in perspectivist societies are deceiving: we never know what we are looking at. While the perspectivist character of some images can be read metaphorically, in other examples the idea that beings can assume different identities is built into the objects' form, where the interdependence of some features means that you must view the object from different angles to reveal the full picture.

COLIMA TOMB DOG
Artefacts, such as this example dating from 200 BCE–500 CE, are common among the burial goods found in the tombs of ancient societies from Western Mexico. Even today, Indigenous Mexicans believe in *naguales* (from the Nahuatl word for shape-shifters), and the notion of an animal double, or *tonal*, is clearly expressed in this statue of a dog wearing a human mask.

KWAKWAKA'WAKW TRANSFORMATION MASK
Myths are replete with creatures shedding their skin to reveal their true natures. Pacific Northwest transformation masks, which depict two overlapping creatures, remind people of the deceiving nature of appearances. They are used to ceremonially re-enact oral traditions, as moral tales and as philosophical reflections on the nature of reality.

SANTARÉM CARYATID VESSEL
Lavishly decorated, this Santarém vessel (1000–1400 CE) from Pará, Brazil, displays what at first sight appear to be unidentifiable figures. Looking closely, these caryatids are ambiguous beings whose plural identities, hidden between shared features, such as eyes, limbs or tails, are only revealed by carefully changing the observer's point of view.

TAÍNO PENDANT
Pre-Columbian Taíno art often features use of parallax, where the viewer's position affects the way they see an object. On this 13th–15th-century pendant a humanoid face is flanked by limbs that appear to be part of the central figure's body, yet belong to two symmetrically positioned figures. This suggests that, by changing appearances, beings change their perspective.

DORSET SHAMAN'S TUBE
The composition of this object from the Dorset culture, of two intertwined walruses on top of an anthropomorphic face, indicates a perspectivist visual approach. The antiquity of this shamanic tube (c. 1000 CE) reveals that ideas about the personhood of animals, other-than-human agency and shape-shifting are very old. Such concepts were transmitted to the Inuit, descendants of the Dorset people.

PANAMA JAR
Hammerhead sharks, manta rays and caymans intertwine in the split representation that decorates this pre-Columbian jar from Panama. This visual strategy allows the viewer to see, across a central axis, two figures that share certain features: the central figure and the one whose half mouth is visible in the profile of the characters on either side of the split.

47 FOUNDATIONS —1— *Animistic Models of the Cosmos*

Young Yanomami preparing for a ceremony, Venezuela, 2005
The central figure is painted with the marks of the jaguar, an important shamanic animal and protagonist of oral traditions. Shamans are said to be able to see the world through the eyes of this animal.

visible and invisible planes. The multiverse is another central principle of animistic lifeways, but there are substantial variations in how societies conceive of it. Notwithstanding differences in the number of layers, the most common cosmological model is one that develops vertically along a main axis, conventionally called by a Latin name: *axis mundi* ('pillar of the world'). This can be imagined to be a tree, a pole, a rope or a set of communicating holes (one example of a cosmological model can be seen on pages 120–21).

Despite its Christian legacy, the term 'animism' has entered current parlance, and Tylor's definition has been adopted in dictionaries and encyclopaedias across the world ever since. Though it went unchallenged for several decades, by the end of the 1980s anthropological research in various areas of the world began to radically reshape the ways in which we think about animism.

New research has shown that, rather than seeing nature as separated from culture, societies in which animism is prevalent tend to see a continuum between species we consider natural. Animals and humans,

Michael Oppitz, *Villagers Returning to Tree of Reincarnation*, Nepal, 1984
This Nepalese shaman perched on a tall pole epitomizes the ascent to the upper world along the cosmic tree, a concept found in several shamanic traditions.

for example, may share interiority, and differing bodily forms produce a different perspective on the world. This is what is called 'perspectivism'. In this model, animals see themselves as cultural beings organized socially, who dwell in specific territories, hunt and eat just as humans do. This notion has been widely recognized among many Indigenous American peoples, from the Arctic to the Amazon, but this outlook is not universal on the continent, and less so across the world, although parallels can be found in different regions. While all societies in which perspectivism is the base of knowledge formation are animist, not all societies that share an animistic worldview can be said to adopt perspectivism.

Nonetheless, as a form of animism, perspectivism shares with it the belief that humans and other species have agency, even what Western observers may consider inert matter, such as rocks, minerals and stones. The animacy that is recognized in natural phenomena – the changing of the seasons, or plant growth – can be more appropriately attributed to a permeating vital force that is present in everything that humans

DECODING THE LION-PERSON

This 40,000-year-old mammoth ivory figurine was named the *Löwenmensch* ('Lion-person') due to its part-human, part-animal character, something that is usually associated with shamanic iconography. It shares certain traits with other Palaeolithic, as well as more recent, representations in which human and animal traits merge. Some believe that it is a naturalistic depiction of a ritual specialist wearing regalia modelled on a lion. Alternative interpretations maintain that this may be a metaphorical representation in which human and animal traits are juxtaposed to convey the idea of transformation central to shamanism, or perhaps that the dual nature depicts what could be described as a mythical creature. Palaeolithic art may have used composite figures to convey complex meanings that escape us today.

1.

HEAD
The feline head has not been positively identified as belonging to either a male or a female lion. It may even show a human wearing a lion's head. This ambiguity makes it difficult to interpret the figurine.

4.

GENITALS
There is much debate about this figurine's se. Some see in the triang flat panel covering the groin area the mark of genitals, while others h suggested it represent female anatomy.

2.

ADORNMENT
The object's poor state of conservation does not allow us to tell whether the figure is wearing any clothing, although the left upper arm displays signs that may indicate decoration or tattoos.

5.

STANCE
The figure is standing like a human, which may suggest this is a human wearing a mask or alternatively a feline *acting* like a human or i the process of changin into a human.

3.

ARMS
Slightly bent and held close to the body, the figure's upper limbs resemble a lion's front legs more than human arms. They end in large cat paws, in keeping with the other feline features of its body.

6.

FEET
The Lion-person appe to have human feet an stands slightly on his t His knees, calves, ankl and heels are also hum like. This complicates interpretations of the figure as a standing lio

51   FOUNDATIONS —1— *Animistic Models of the Cosmos*

Yup'ik shamanic mask, Alaska, *c.* 1900
This mask is composed of parts of different beings. Shamans can conjure up and manage multiple beings at once, but the mask may also be a representation of transformation.

Yup'ik caribou-human mask, Alaska, 19th century
The human legs belonging to the caribou depicted on this mask may indicate its personhood or the ability to shape-shift that is common in several shamanic traditions.

experience. The idea that humans partake of the same powerful energy that gives life to the cosmos is another of the central tenets of an animistic worldview.

There are great differences between animistic models, particularly in the emphasis put on the types of relationships that may be forged between species, between humans and natural elements, or between humans and intangible beings. For example, Mongolian animism strongly emphasizes the relationship between humans and the sky, Tengri. In most South American societies, by contrast, the focus is on human–animal relationships, especially jaguar–human interactions, and the significance given to ancestral spirits among South East Asian forest peoples is different again. All these peoples believe in a world in which species can communicate through different layers of reality, and sometimes even change into one another. However, while Mongolian-speaking peoples do not expect to become the sky, Amazonian Indigenous peoples consider the possibility that jaguars and humans can adopt each other's point of view or even transform into one another, and mediums in, for example, South East Asia even temporarily welcome into their bodies spirits from the land of the dead.

Shamanic practitioners during the annual Blue Pearl Ice Festival, Lake Khövsgöl, Mongolia, 2019
In Mongolia, communication with the invisible inhabitants of the cosmos may take the form of ritualized interactions mediated by prayers and invocations.

The extent to which certain peoples personify distinctive entities, be it the sky, a jaguar or a dead relative, is an important factor in establishing differences and similarities between animistic models. Elements such as the sky may not qualify to be persons, but many other visible and invisible entities may. Whether temporarily or permanently, some things that humans know and experience may be conceived of and talked about as 'persons', and their ability to influence the world of the living with their actions and whimsical behaviours qualifies them as 'human-like'. Current scholarship has come up with a neutral definition for these diverse agents, without any direct referent to organized religions: they are described as 'other-than-human persons'. They may be bears in Siberia, certain stones among Native North Americans, jaguars in the Amazonian jungles, insects in the Arctic or incorporeal entities that interfere with humans everywhere in the world.

This notion of personhood emerged from an empirical acknowledgment of the relational nature of the world, one in which interactions between

Shamanic healing ceremony from Simona Piantieri's documentary *Shamans and the City*, 2025
A shamanic practitioner performs a healing ceremony in a London park. Contemporary urban shamanism is inspired by different traditions, as in this case, which is inspired by Mexican Huichol shamanism.

humans and others are foundational for maintaining balance and equilibrium in the cosmos. The existence of these connections may at times be visualized as a network that expands in all directions, for example among the Shipibo-Conibo of Peru, who conceive of the universe as a mesh that envelops everything and everyone.

Recognizing that the world may be animated by many types of 'persons' means that, in the animistic universe, humans are not the only ones endowed with the prerogatives of intentionality, decision-making and choice. All persons may act according to their own logic, and therefore animistic thought assigns cause and effect to events in the world in ways that are different from the mechanical models proposed by science.

The substantial divergences between animistic models and scientific ones may render a reconciliation between them difficult. Yet, contemporary shamans and their followers do not see any contradiction in straddling the two, both in daily life and in ceremonial practice. This is particularly pronounced in modern industrialized contexts, where shamans now frequently

Mircea Eliade, 1978
Romanian historian of religion Mircea Eliade is considered to be the father of shamanic studies in the West. His seminal work, Shamanism: Archaic Techniques of Ecstasy *(first published in French in 1951), has for many years been the most authoritative book on the matter among Western scholars.*

Edward Burnett Tylor, c. 1900
Edward Burnett Tylor belonged to a generation of positivist intellectuals who posited that animist thinking was misguided and 'primitive'. Contrary to predictions that science would slowly replace belief, animist worldviews, including those that underpin shamanism, have today been resurrected around the world.

operate. From Ulaanbaatar in Mongolia to Sedona in Arizona, customary and syncretic forms of shamanism, which have emerged over the last few decades, negotiate between often incompatible models of the world, the universe and the cosmos, establishing new relationships between the environment and its inhabitants, be they human or other-than-human. These inhabitants include not only plants and animals, but also what the West would perceive as inanimate objects, such as mountains, forests, the water in rivers and lakes, and even the air and the weather.

In these scenarios, animistic worldviews appear to provide alternative explanations of the world's inner workings, and – for most Western audiences – a window into ecological issues. The strong bonds between humans and animals and all living things promoted by an animistic worldview puts into sharp focus the disconnection that most contemporary urban dwellers feel between themselves and the environment, or what in more generic terms they perceive to be the realm of 'nature'. The appeal of animism for today's urbanized, globalized populations is enormous, and it is generally filtered through the lens of shamanism. The popularity of animism can be seen by the ever-expanding network of workshops, seminars, publications and websites dedicated to shamanic healing, training and practice.

Much of what is commercially available, however, is tinted with a veneer of romanticism that offers only a partial understanding of the complexities of, and differences between, animistic worldviews and attitudes. Most notably, it tends to focus on the positive, healing and restorative aspects of shamanic practices embedded in animistic lifeworlds. What frequently remains marginal in the presentation of animism to Western audiences are the dark, predatory and negative facets that are intrinsic to animistic models. These are for the most part dualistic, in that they posit a cosmos that is positive and yet simultaneously inhabited by negative forces and by people who want to do evil. In these models, shamans are essential to solve the issues that arise from the ongoing tensions created by the opposing forces. Not coincidentally, animistic cosmic geographies postulate the existence of areas of the universe populated by good entities, and others that are inhabited by malevolent ones.

Not all animistic models, however, reflect this rigid structure for understanding and explaining the world. Some may flexibly incorporate changes and nuances into the ways in which they conceive of the cosmos and its inhabitants. While in some places entities may be essentially good or bad, in others humans and other-than-human persons may be neither good nor bad, but simply act in ways that align with their own viewpoints. In perspectivist modes of animism the model changes further. In the Amazon, jaguars may see humans as prey, but their behaviour is not evil per se. It is a question of perspective; jaguars may also perceive humans as predators, which at times they are. In this approach, evil and good exist as relative moral conditions, and nothing is fundamentally either one or the other. Circumstances may dictate a person's perception, and this is why a position of suspicion and circumspection is the required default in the intimately interrelated animistic world.

Siona shaman, Ecuador, 2013

Some Tukanoan-speaking peoples of South America, including the Siona, follow shamanic models based on ideas of predation or reciprocity that structure their cosmology and belief systems. Anthropologists have noted that shamanistic models based on predation are more likely to be associated with hunting and gathering groups.

PROFILE
ANIMALS

In the shamanic world, animals play a central role. Whether helpers or predators, they are often considered other-than-human persons that interact with humans. Each animal is associated with unique behaviours or abilities. Some species are attributed more powers than others, and ritual and ceremonial complexes have developed around the knowledge produced about them through myths, legends, lore and empirical experience. The importance of specific animals is reflected in the frequency with which they appear in the visual culture of certain regions, but also in sacrificial contexts, where their remains are left visible on purpose-made shrines and ritual structures, and even burials, where one can see the respect with which they are treated. Birds are particularly significant as they are often seen as messengers, guides or metaphors for shamanic flight and cosmic soul journeys. Their forms regularly feature on shamanic apparel and musical instruments, as amulets and sculptures, and as motifs in rock art, as can be seen in these pictographs in Cueva Pintada, Baja California, Mexico.

DEER
Among several Indigenous Mexican societies, including the one in Nayarit that produced this Chinesco figure (100 BCE–300 CE), the deer has a cosmological significance that has its roots in the mysterious workings of the universe and connects the deer to shamanism. It is associated with a shamanic complex in which the sun, peyote and hunt converge, and is honoured in dances and the visual arts.

CROCODILES
In tropical regions of South and Central America, crocodilian figures represent aggression. In pre-Columbian times crocodile masks were worn by shamans, and, in the cultures of Costa Rica, shamans were sometimes portrayed in the process of becoming crocodiles, sitting on their ceremonial stools. This Costa Rican vessel dating from 1000–1521 CE would have been used to burn incense.

FROGS
Amazonian *muiraquitã* are often carved into the shape of frogs, like this *c.* 1300 CE example from Brazil. Some frog species are known to secrete a psychotropic substance from their skin. It is used by some shamans to alter their ordinary consciousness. Their amphibian life places frogs between terrestrial and aquatic environments, making them – like the shaman – intermediaries between worlds.

HORSES
Siberian and Central Asian shamanic cultures attributed great importance to horses. They were elaborately adorned in life, as demonstrated by this Pazyryk mask (600–200 BCE) made for a horse, and were given dignified burials at death. Horses were occasionally sacrificed to accompany their masters in the afterlife, and among societies of the Altai Mountains they were spirit protectors.

JAGUARS
Representations of felines date back to early prehistory. Jaguars, pumas, ocelots and other cats embody ideas of predation, strength, aggression, swiftness and ferocity. Highly regarded in most Amerindian shamanic societies, jaguars are among the animals that shamans most frequently change into. This Ecuadorian greenstone Chorrera mortar depicts a jaguar and dates from 1200–300 BCE.

BEARS
Bear cults associated with shamanism exist across North America, Siberia, China and Eastern Europe. Made by the Koryak people of Siberia, this tobacco pipe is decorated with carved polar bears. Of all animals in Siberia, bears most closely resemble human behaviour, gait and posture. They are the quintessential other-than-human person that displays agency, intentionality and intelligence.

59   FOUNDATIONS −1− *Animistic Models of the Cosmos*

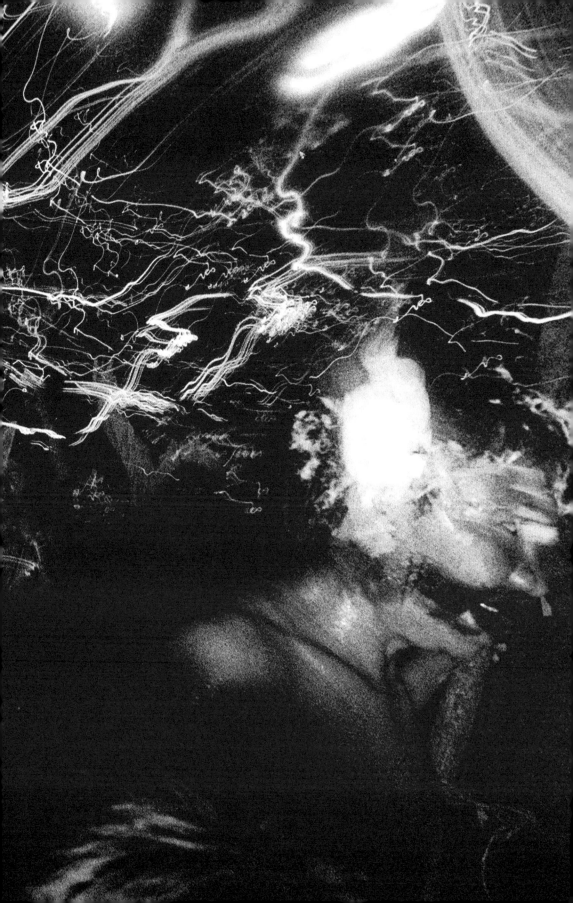

SHAMANIC PRACTICE IN AN ANIMISTIC COSMOS

'I have come to ask about the heavy suffering, /
I am asking a great favour, / I want to know the command of
the khans, / I am looking for the runaway soul, / Let me comb
your golden hair, / Let me comb your silver hair, / Let me in!'

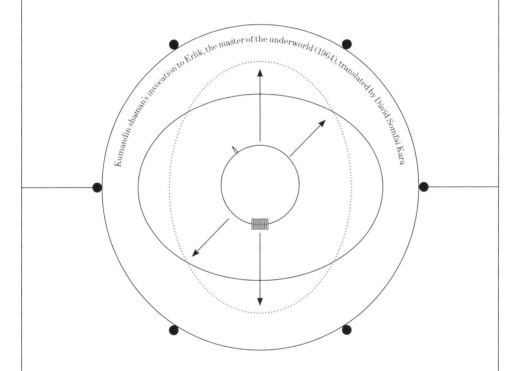

Kumandin shaman's invocation to Erlik, the master of the underworld (1964), translated by David Somfai Kara

Shamans solve their communities' problems through direct
engagement with visible beings and invisible entities, which they
summon through rituals and ceremonies. Mustering a variety of skills,
shamans are often aided by human helpers or other-than-human tutelary
beings that support them through their ordeals and spiritual battles.
Witnesses tell of wondrous feats of magic, which shamans explain
as spiritual power. Their elaborate rituals have fascinated both
casual eyewitnesses and scientific observers.

Living in an animistic cosmos means attempting to maintain good relations with everything in the world: from plants and animals to stones and weather phenomena, from mountains and rivers to the entities that inhabit them. Members of animistic societies tend to follow routine practices through which they acknowledge the reciprocal obligations that humans and other-than-human beings hold towards each other on both the visible and the invisible planes. By and large, societies in which animism plays a part in interpreting reality recognize the limits of human power over both the natural and supernatural worlds.

Prayers, invocations and offerings regularly performed by individuals and communities are pacts sealed between them and the beings with which they share a common world. This behaviour – marked by conventional gestures, cyclical rituals and ceremonies – simultaneously marks an agreement and establishes a moral code. It is a constant reminder of the duties that each entity has towards the others; duties which, if contravened, may cause a disruption in the delicate balance that must be maintained between cosmic forces through collective effort. Immoral actions, disobeying a proscription or breaking an agreement with other-than-human beings may enrage and upset those beings, causing a crisis that requires specialist intervention.

Handling these complex and delicate interactions is a responsibility that often falls upon shamans, who try to counteract the unpredictability of whimsical beings' agreements with humans, or mend the damage done by unruly persons. Sickness, epidemics, psychological troubles, diseases and even minor ailments may be caused by contravening the responsibilities that each person has towards other beings. Among Korean followers of shamanism, difficult relationships with the ancestors may necessitate the intervention of shamans, who will remedy the affliction by establishing the gifts that the affected family must offer to the spirits to appease them. In Peru, when a Shipibo-Conibo person falls sick, it may be seen as a punishment for not following social customs. Only shamans can undo the

⟨ pages 60–61
Claudia Andujar,
'Yanomami in Catrimani, Brazil', from the series
O reahu, 1974
The light effects in this evocative photograph conjure up images of otherworldly realms inhabited by the entities Yanomami shamans interact with.

⟨ page 62
Witchcraft, Sitka, Alaska, c. 1885
This staged studio photograph illustrates a Haida shaman subduing a 'witch', an evil-doer who uses their power to cause harm.

A. Abbas, shaman conducting a ceremony for a dead couple, Seoul, South Korea, 1998

Ensuring that spirits rest in peace after death is a responsibility of shamans. This is an extension of their role as a guide of souls in the afterlife. Money, shown here tucked into the shaman's headdress, is frequently used as an offering to certain gods or as payment for the shaman's services.

65 FOUNDATIONS — 2 — *Shamanic Practice in an Animistic Cosmos*

DECODING PONCE MONOLITH

Recent interpretations of this imposing monument from the Tiwanaku culture (600–1000 CE) reveal undeniable links to shamanic practices and ideologies. The hybrid nature of the being represented and the rich iconography that decorates its body show the extent of shamanic influences on this visual culture. It is not known exactly how the statue was used nor who it represents, whether an ancestral shaman, a mythical figure or a deity. It was found in the courtyard of a structure known as the Kalasasaya at the Tiwanaku site in Bolivia.

1.

ANIMAL-HEADED HELPERS
The headband is engraved with depictions of staff-bearing helpers. They have either feline, fish or bird heads. Similar helpers are carved into other monuments at the same site, most notably the sun gate.

2.

TEARS
Tears are a common motif in American shamanic cultures, but tears that end in fish heads are unique to Tiwanaku. Tears are associated with the ingestion of psychotropic plants and seeds that provoke discharges of bodily fluids.

3.

SNUFF TABLET
The kind of object held by this figure is unique to the Americas, where snuff (made from pulverized plants, vines, seeds and leaves, mixed with lime and other activating substances) is inhaled from tablets to help the user reach an ASC.

4.

KERO
This type of ceremonial beaker has been used for libations and offerings throughout the pre-Columbian period, and continues to be used today. It may contain maize beer, water or blood. Offerings are common in many forms of shamanism.

5.

SEEDS
The concentric circles in this pattern have been interpreted as representations of vilca seeds, which are used in shamanic rituals for their psychotropic properties. Similar iconography is common in neighbouring cultures, such as the Diaguita.

6.

FELINE FEET
The appearance of paws on a human figure is usually characteristic of shape-shifting. The individual represented might be in a state of transformation, or the feline feet may simply be a metaphor for the mighty power of a shaman.

Hmong shaman Wang Pao Yang during a healing ceremony in Fresno, California, 2009
Acceptance of alternative healing practices and religious pluralism has meant an increase in the shamanic presence in Western hospitals and care institutions.

Lelooska, *Oyster Catcher Rattle*, Washington, c. 1970
The scene depicted on this shamanic rattle by an Indigenous North American artist resembles the scene photographed on page 62. The shaman is taming his opponent, possibly aided by a mountain goat's medicine, transmitted through the animal's tongue.

damage by restoring the luminous and fragrant net that envelops the individual and which only they can see.

Scientific thought makes a distinction between disease (abnormalities of the function and/or structure of the body) and illness (the subjective experience of ill health), and shamans frequently deal with pathologies both of the body and of the soul (or souls, depending on beliefs), though they would argue that the two are linked. They can be herbalists and doctors as well as healers. This means using methods that act on their clients physiologically as well as psychosomatically. Although some are sceptical of shamans' ability to effect permanent cures, the highly dramatic, performative healing sessions staged for the benefit of a patient have often been deemed successful, as in the case of Hmong shamans curing cancer.

Shamanic healing can take many forms, but practitioners everywhere operate holistically as both doctors and psychological counsellors. Spiritual healing is augmented by botanical knowledge as well as a strong dose of belief in the shaman's ability to restore wellness and health. Because physical ailments always have a spiritual component, shamans cannot simply cure the symptoms, they must go to the source of the disease, which is always spiritual in nature. For example, they might travel to the subterranean realms to retrieve

68   FOUNDATIONS — 2 — *Shamanic Practice in an Animistic Cosmos*

Achuar shaman cleansing an elected deputy, Ecuador, 2003
Some shamans blow their protective power into the patient's head at the point where the bones of the skull meet, ridding them of undesired invisible presences.

a person's soul if it has been stolen by malevolent spirits; or gallop into the cracks of mountains to talk to the beings that dwell therein. In hunting societies shamans also deal with the masters of animals, or the chiefs of certain species. Because shamans are the only ones who can speak their language, their role is to convince the masters of animals to release the animals under their power. In other circumstances, shamans also have the ability to fight wicked ghosts with invisible darts. The most dire situations may necessitate meeting the lords of the underworld, as in the Siberian invocation at the beginning of this chapter aimed at restoring health in a sick individual.

Shamans intercede on behalf of humans, pleading with other beings for their forgiveness in exchange for respect or regular libations, or asking for permission to use the territories over which they preside. They act as mediators, making deals with invisible forces, or evil counterparts. No one can fight spiritual attacks, nor extract a confession from an alleged witch as competently as a shaman. Some of these interactions may require formulaic procedures that cut across

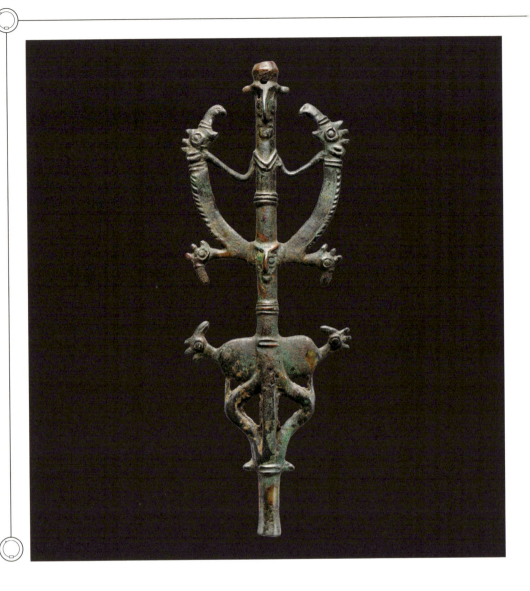

PROFILE
MASTERS AND MISTRESSES OF ANIMALS

The notion of a master or mistress of animals is very ancient and exists in many cultures. They are figures, most often mythical or intangible, who wield a particular power over specific animal species. The extent to which masters of animals can be interpreted as shamans and their helpers or simply as individuals who work with shamans has not yet been resolved, but the two iconographies bear distinct similarities. This Iron Age Iranian bronze (c. 800–600 BCE), probably from Luristan, may represent a master of animals or perhaps a shaman with helpers.

SCYTHIAN PENDANT
The animals governed by a master may be of the same species or of different species. They might be hybrid creatures, which may be linked to shamanism or mythology. In shamanic iconography, animals may sit on the shaman's arms or shoulders. This 25–50 CE pendant from Tillya Tepe, Afghanistan, shows a similar composition.

COLOMBIAN BREASTPLATE
The master or mistress is always flanked by animals or other beings. This is similar to representations of shamans and their helpers. The central figure may be sitting, standing or moving, but a hierarchical composition is always upheld, as can be seen in this 900–1600 CE depiction of a shaman from Cauca, Colombia.

GUNDESTRUP CAULDRON
The head has an important symbolic role, because its decorations usually identify the character as a special person. Horned bands, caps or unique headdresses change from place to place. This famous figure from the interior of the Gundestrup cauldron (150–1 BCE), found in Denmark, has antlers.

AGUADA PLAQUE
Most images of masters or mistresses of animals use a symmetrical composition for maximum visual impact, including this plaque (450–900 CE) from the Aguada culture of Argentina. This mode of representation has been called 'iconic'. It is widely associated with religious imagery.

ÇATALHÖYÜK FIGURINE
In some regions, such as the Mediterranean and tropical Central and South America, women may be represented as mistresses of animals. Whether standing or sitting, they grab onto their animals' necks, as can be seen in this c. 6000 BCE terracotta figurine from Çatalhöyük, Turkey.

GREATER NICOYA FIGURINE
Sometimes mistresses of animals or women shamans are depicted sitting on thrones or stools flanked by animals. They also may be sitting on them as a marker of power and divination, as can be seen in this 800–1200 CE female figure from Greater Nicoya, Costa Rica, who sits on a bench with felines.

Mongolian shaman brothers, Ulaanbaatar, Mongolia, 2012
Mongolian shamanism is deeply entwined with Buddhism. Rituals of gratitude for the spirits of nature may be requested by those who want to accrue good deeds for their karma.

cultural differences (for example, altering one's ordinary perception, or becoming oracles). There are also cultural and temporal variations, however, and these may account for the multifarious ways in which local practitioners develop individual styles and techniques.

Many societies recognize different typologies of shamans: those that deal with magic and necromancy; those that deal with healing; and those that manage the affairs of the hunt, or of divination. Clearly, each of these specializations requires specific techniques and rituals. For divination purposes, eighteenth-century Saami shamans (*noaidi*) consulted the icons on their drums, but ancient Chinese shamans (*wu*) interpreted marks incised on bones and tortoise shells. Amazonian shamans (*paje*) may need to adjust their consciousness to see into the future, as the *völvas* from medieval Scandinavia did.

In some regions shamans may have special ties to certain occupations, for example blacksmiths, with whom they share the knowledge required to change matter. Among the Buryat of south-eastern Siberia, shamans perform rituals for blacksmiths, who in turn

Healing session, West Kalimantan, Indonesia, 2012

Helpers are supporting a shaman in a trance. Indonesian healers are usually called dukun, *a term that has negative connotations in some regions for its association with the ability to cause harm. In general, it describes an individual with exceptional qualities, including the ability to see the future, heal, and communicate with the dead.*

make the instruments and accoutrements the shamans need. Though not all shamans develop relationships with specialists in other areas, they do establish lasting ties with their human helpers. Apprentices, and at times their spouses, assist shamans in their rituals by making sure that all the necessary material is available and sustaining the practitioner during trances by providing water and physical support. Sometimes the sessions require that shamans be tied or restrained to prevent them from harming themselves when they lapse into a dangerous dissociative state.

By and large, shamans operate on a one-to-one basis, but they also perform in front of their patients' family and kin, or take part in communal rituals. Such public spectacles of shamanic abilities not only confirm a shaman's powers in the eyes of the observers, but also underline the importance of respecting social norms for the benefit of the group, and may help to resolve community tensions or interpersonal frictions.

Shamans' ritual and ceremonial lives are punctuated by numerous activities that establish their reputations and their credibility in the community. Their public

Shaking Tent, Lac du Flambeau, Wisconsin

The Anishinaabe, like several neighbouring groups, hold 'Shaking Tent' ceremonies for healing and divination. The structure is built from branches and covered on all sides (except the open top) with bark or, in more recent times, cotton or muslin to allow privacy for the shaman undergoing a trance.

recognition is sealed by the extraordinary things they can do. Appearing to inflict wounds and injuries without shedding blood, or freeing themselves from intricate bindings, are among the most common acts performed by shamans as proof of their exceptional powers.

Among the Cree and Ojibwa First Nations in Canada, and in a local variation among Sioux nations in the USA, a ceremony called the 'Shaking Tent' is regularly held to consult the invisible forces on matters of health, hunting and even to identify wrongdoers. The shaman is tied up inside a purpose-built tent, which is then wrapped closed, apart from an opening at the top enabling the *manitous*, the intangible entities that will commune with the shaman, to be called inside. From here he delivers his verdicts, which he translates from his conversations with spirit beings summoned by him, and who are usually heard screeching, howling or making terrifying noises inside the structure. This great commotion (the 'Shaking') is usually followed by silence. When the ceremony is over the assistants open the tent to reveal the untied shaman lying on the ground, exhausted from the strenuous effort.

Unlike priests, rabbis, brahmins, imams and other ritual specialists, shamans do not operate within organized clerical structures. No hierarchies are formally recognized among them, but age, expertise and demonstrable efficacy account for substantial differences between practitioners. Other ceremonialists who run rituals, liturgies and rites may differentiate along the lines of gender or social position (such as caste or elite lineage), but in the small-scale societies in which many shamans conduct their work these social coordinates must be situated in an animistic context. This means acknowledging how different shamanisms reflect and at the same time shape the socio-cultural formations in which they are embedded. The egalitarian view of the world in which many shamans perform their duties allows shamans to contact the invisible worlds directly without having to pass through a long line of intermediaries, as may happen in, for example, the Catholic Church or Hinduism, where at best the worshipper can hope to be seen by the manifestation

DECODING SHAMANIC HEALING

Healing sessions are among the most dramatic displays of shamanic power. Various accoutrements can be used to facilitate this practice, some of which are pictured in this 1886–90 reconstruction of an Alaskan Haida shaman's healing practice. Though the form and content of these sessions vary, there are some elements that are similar cross-culturally. Musical accompaniment, often using instruments, is the most common element. Songs, humming, invocations and prayers regularly feature as an essential part of the process and may be used to communicate with invisible forces and entities. In some regions, masks and special accoutrements are used to facilitate the soul's journey if an ASC is required. Helpers always assist shamans during these sessions.

1. SETTING
Shamanic seances normally happen in domestic interiors, but in this case a healing session has been reconstructed in a photographic studio to document the practice. This staged image may give us the closest possible representation of the reality of a Haida shaman's practice, even if the healer had long stopped his practice. Although the image reproduces an Indigenous Alaskan scene, objects seen in this picture are common to shamans everywhere.

2. HEADDRESS
Headdresses, such as the one shown here, have a special function in shamanic practice. When made of moving parts or decorated with pendants or spangles, they produce sounds and vibrations that help shamans to achieve trance states. They can work as technologies of communication between phenomenal reality and invisible dimensions. Usually, they have antennae-like extensions that resemble, or are made of, antlers, horns, branches or feathers.

3. MASK
Some shamans of this region used masks for curing and healing, hence the inclusion of a mask in this staged image, but not all shamans do. Masks associated with shamanic practice are found in areas including the Pacific Northwest, Canada and Siberia among the Altaic peoples. Decline in mask use is linked to prohibitions, for example the Mongol–Oirat code of 1640 that banned shamanism in Asian territories that had converted to Buddhism.

4. IMPLEMENTS
Uncommonly, this shaman holds a dagger, the use of which might have been dictated by the availability of props to stage the scene. In real seances, shamans may use invisible weapons or miniature replicas to protect themselves against malevolent forces. Though shamans may tailor their practice to their unique preferences, often musical instruments, batons, sucking tubes, charms, crystals and feathers help them to achieve their goals.

5. CLOAK
Cloaks, coats, ponchos, mantles and capes are the shaman's protective armour. Here the shaman is dressed in what appears to be a painted skin, in keeping with the region's traditions. Garments such as this are decorated with images of spirits, animal helpers and other entities familiar to the practising shaman. Everywhere in the world shamans use personal objects decorated with images from dreams, visions or spiritual encounters for protection.

6. AMULETS
Under the shaman's left hand is a large necklace decorated with pendants made of animal teeth, carved bone and antler. Such powerful objects are worn by the shaman, but if needed they may be rubbed against the patient to release their healing properties or donated to them for everlasting protection. In shamanic thinking some materials contain substances that help to cure. Only shamans know the right combinations to achieve total recovery.

77   FOUNDATIONS — 2 — *Shamanic Practice in an Animistic Cosmos*

Shamans, Gyeonggi-do, South Korea, 2007
Becoming a shaman may entail initiation rituals and years of apprenticeship. Here the trainees perform a rite to demonstrate their shamanic abilities after being possessed by spirits. There are substantial differences between hereditary shamanism and an individual calling to the profession. This ritual is one way potential shamans may display their vocation.

of a deity. In Islam, no one except the prophets can come into direct contact with the divine. By contrast, in an animistic framework, everyone potentially can do so, although there may be differences between those that experience only occasional spiritual encounters and those, like shamans, who specialize in this type of communication.

Though interaction with metaphysical realities forms a great part of shamans' work, their relationship with the visible world is equally as important. Shamans will, therefore, perform rituals for the rivers, mountains and atmospheric elements. Because of their deep knowledge of how all beings behave, they may also draw upon their botanical and zoological knowledge.

Notwithstanding the important contribution they offer their communities, shamans and their families are frequently kept at a distance. This is because they are ambivalent figures who deal with powerful and often dangerous forces that, if mismanaged, can put the whole community at grave risk.

While the occupation may be hereditary, as in the case of Mongolians, Buryats and Kyrgyz, in most cases shamans are selected for special qualities, perhaps behaviours recognized early in childhood, or are directly summoned by spiritual entities during out-of-the-ordinary events such as visions, apparitions or

José Benítez Sánchez, *The Dismemberment of Takusi Nakawé*, 1973
The mythical scene depicted in this Huichol yarn painting encapsulates the shamanic notion that dismemberment is an act of regeneration. Shamans undergo this ordeal before being reborn as healers.

powerful recurring dreams experienced at some point in their lives. It is not uncommon to hear that an individual became a shaman following a life crisis, a near-death experience or a traumatic event. Frequently, these episodes involve an encounter with the intangible realms and their inhabitants, including demons or malevolent spirits that may even 'dismember' the dreamer during terrifying spiritual ordeals.

Yet, even if a child is born to become a shaman because of certain diagnostic traits or hereditary rights, each individual must still learn the arts of the profession. Acquiring the knowledge necessary to act as a shaman is indispensable. The world of the unknown, with which the shaman will regularly deal, is full of unexpected circumstances, and the appropriate techniques and solutions must be understood and applied.

Shamans have rituals related to childbirth, for ridding spaces of unwanted entities, and for accompanying the dead to the underworld. They have ceremonies for making offerings to the spirits of nature, for providing blessings and for returning wandering souls to ailing patients. Most of these rituals include songs, dances,

PROFILE
OFFERINGS AND SACRIFICES

In the context of shamanism, the covenant sought between humans and incorporeal entities is sealed by acts of reciprocity, most frequently marked by offerings and sometimes by sacrifices. Some followers may dedicate objects dear to them to the spirits of ancestors, while others following customary practice offer what they know pleases certain entities. This Mongolian *ovoo*, or cairn, for example, is topped with blue silk offerings to Tengri, the sky. Usually, offerings are accompanied by chants or impromptu prayers, which in some cases may be materialized in objects left on or near shrines.

FOOD
Food may be left as offerings in Eastern forms of shamanism. Impressive displays of abundance left on shamanic altars indicate that humans received the help they asked for from the invisible entities consulted by the shaman.

LIBATIONS
Liquid offerings – libations – have been reported in the context of shamanic rituals since antiquity. Supplicants might use milk, alcohol and even, in the past, blood to ingratiate themselves with spirits and other-than-human entities.

SMOKE
Smoke plays a part in many shamanic rituals. It has healing properties and, as an offering, it is believed to be pleasing to the spirits and bring human prayers up to the higher levels of the cosmos where certain incorporeal entities live.

FLESH
Self-sacrifice was practised in many Amerindian shamanic cultures: north Mexican Indigenous people drew blood in peyote rituals, and some Native American men took part in flesh offerings or piercing rituals, as is imitated in this staged photograph.

ANIMALS
Animal sacrifices are rather common in shamanic ceremonial life. Depending on local availability, pigs, horses, reindeer or llamas may be among the most precious gifts offered by individuals or communities.

PRAYERS
In some places, prayers are materialized in special objects such as incense or sticks, like the ones being left by the Huichol people pictured here. They are the visible sign of believers' presence and a token of their commitment to the spirit world.

FOUNDATIONS — 2 — *Shamanic Practice in an Animistic Cosmos*

invocations or unintelligible sounds from secret languages. These ritual elements are not simple accompaniments to the ceremony, but are essential for the success of the rites because of the power attributed to words and gestures.

Part of shamans' ceremonial repertoire may also include their participation in public rites. Many shamans today are called upon to perform rituals beyond their customary operations in the realm of healing, curing, restoring cosmic balance or speaking to the dead, especially for ceremonies established with the purpose of rooting national identities into past religions and beliefs. Nativistic movements, such as those that have sprung up recently in Eastern Europe, employ the language of shamanism in their reconstruction of ancient cults such as those of sun and birch worship. These are run by shamans called *volkhv* among Slavic-speaking adherents of a modern pagan religion known as Rodnovery (Native Faith). In places such as Ukraine, Russia and the Czech Republic, but also in Finno-Ugric regions such as Estonia, Finland, Hungary and the Russian autonomous regions of Mari El and Udmurtia, Neo-Pagan or Indigenous movements that reject the Christian faith typically maintain that the figure of the shaman pre-dates that of the priest. Consequently, despite inevitable regional differences, shamans have re-entered the context of religious festivals and of celebrations that are associated with old beliefs, for example harvest festivals, solstices and equinoxes.

Lately, shamans have begun coming together for large international occasions such as the International Gathering of Shamans, the Annual International Shamanic Conference, or the Call of 13 Shamans held in Tuva, Siberia, whose objective is to raise global awareness of environmentalism, shamanism and various spiritual matters. The reframing of shamans as activists is a new phenomenon that by far exceeds the roles once assigned to them in traditional cultures, but most shamans today, like those of the past, still perform rituals and ceremonies that, while incorporating some changes, fundamentally tend to follow old templates.

> *pages 84–85*
Tuvan shaman spreading milk around a stone altar, Russia, 2003
Shamans use offerings to connect to invisible forces and entities. Such ritual gestures always begin sacred ceremonies and gatherings as a form of blessing.

Roberto Quijada, Buryat shaman, Olkhon Island, Russia, 2005

Shamanic gatherings, such as the Annual International Shamanic Conference on Olkhon Island, Russia, are a recent phenomenon. These are ceremonial occasions where shamans come together to strengthen social relations, renew their covenant with spirits and invisible beings, and pray for the good of humankind.

RELIGIOUS (DIS–) CONNECTIONS

'Hunting shamans was [Commander Henry Glass's] favourite pastime and sport. A captured shaman was usually invited aboard.... Shamans always left his boat with their heads half shaved and covered with oil paint, and having promised not to practise shamanism any more.'

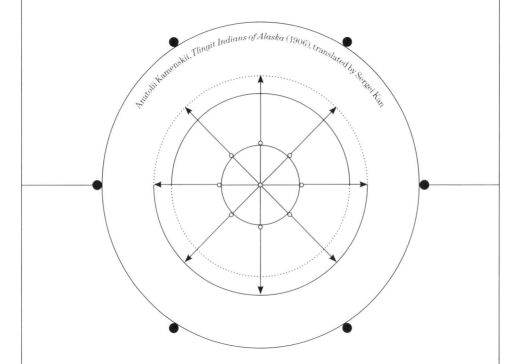

Anatolii Kamenskii, *Tlingit Indians of Alaska* (1906), translated by Sergei Kan

Over the centuries, shamans encountering new religions variably experienced total rejection and persecution, as well as incorporation and syncretism. Interreligious synergies are often noticeable in the visual cultures and ideas that underpin shamans' lives and work. The spread of world religions in large parts of Asia, Europe, the Americas and Africa had a significant impact on shamanism, which changed into a multiplicity of ever-evolving forms that are still visible today.

O ld descriptions of shamans tell us much about the attitudes of the people who met them for the first time. Whether coloured by dismay, surprise, disenchantment, repulsion or sheer disapproval, these accounts reveal the tension between often irreconcilable worldviews. The encounter between different belief systems is a constant theme in human history, and the meetings of shamans with unfamiliar religions is part of that narrative.

Historically, the practice of shamanism has been variably linked to the many faiths it has encountered in the territories where it has traditionally operated. Central Asia, Siberia, the Himalayan region, the Americas, some parts of Africa, as well as Europe: these are all places where shamans have been positively identified, or where echoes of their practices have been recorded.

Shamans' connections to organized religion are most clearly detectable in the Eurasian context, where Hinduism, Zoroastrianism, Buddhism, Bön, Tengrism and Islam have variously crossed paths with the role of shamans and their animistic experience of the world. In other parts of the world, too, such as the Americas and Africa, where Christianity has been more prevalent, shamans have had to contend with new symbols and values, sometimes translating local concepts into the terminology of this imported religion.

Regardless of the degree to which different belief systems impacted each other, inter-faith relationships on all continents point to influences, innovations, suppression, continuities and also syncretism, the process by which elements from different religions or belief systems merge to create something entirely new.

It is not always possible to establish the origins of practices that appear similar in both shamanic and non-shamanic contexts, but correlations between them may indicate areas of common belief or mutual influence, and – in some cases – may be based on direct historical contacts, or geographical proximity. While in many regions these relationships developed gradually through mutual influences (as in the case of Hinduism and Buddhism), the abrupt imposition of entirely new

‹ *page 86*
Bronze figure of Shiva Nataraja (Lord of Cosmic Dance), Tamil Nadu, India, *c.* 930–40 CE
This Hindu god has been variably associated with shamanic roots due to his ascetic practices and association with plants such as datura, which produces psychotropic effects. Datura flowers can be seen adorning this figure's head.

88   FOUNDATIONS — 3 — *Religious (Dis-) Connections*

Essie Parrish (Piwoya), Kashaya Pomo spiritual leader, California, c. 1950

Shaman and healer Essie Parrish was instructed by dreams to decorate her ceremonial regalia with symbols from both Native and Christian traditions. The regalia was worn during ceremonies of the Bole Maru cult, one of several nativistic movements in the American West in the late 19th and early 20th centuries.

FOUNDATIONS — 3 — *Religious (Dis-) Connections*

PROFILE
SHAMANIC ARCHETYPES IN EURASIAN LORE

Psychoanalysis-influenced scholars have searched for shamanic echoes among the recurring themes of Eurasian epic literature, poems, legends and myths. Despite criticism, they seek to prove that there is an ideological substratum shared by Eurasian people from the Bronze Age to the Middle Ages. Albrecht Dürer's 1513 engraving, below, shows the archetypal hero who confronts death. A parallel may be drawn to the distant traditions of shamans, who confront death regularly.

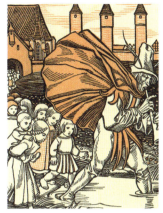

INCANTATION AND MUSIC
Mythical characters such as Orpheus and the Pied Piper of Hamelin, pictured in this German illustration from *c.* 1906, are able to spellbind animals and people through their music and incantations. Characters with these abilities are said to be analogous to the shamanic master of animals.

DESCENDING TO THE UNDERWORLD
Travelling to the realm of the dead is common in shamanic traditions. Therefore, some see Greek mythological figures such as Persephone, who was rescued from Hades by Hermes the psychopomp, as shamanic. This *c.* 440–430 BCE cup shows both Persephone and Hades.

HEALING POTIONS
Potions, elixirs and magical cures that use plants appear frequently in Eurasian myths, folk stories and religious literature. The Zoroastrian divine plant *haoma*, the Vedic drink *soma*, being used here to anoint Indra, and Homer's *nepenthes pharmakon* have all been associated with shamanic psychotropic plants.

NEAR-DEATH EXPERIENCES
Near death or death followed by resurrection are common events in folklore. In the Maria Morevna fairy tale, famously illustrated by Ivan Bilibin, Prince Ivan is cut into pieces by an evil wizard and then revived. Such ordeals are reminiscent of shamans' dismemberment and illness.

TRANSFORMATION
Shape-shifting characters are frequent in stories from all Eurasian language groups. Many wizards, witches and other figures can turn into animals at will, recalling abilities reported for shamans. One such witch, Louhi, is shown in Akseli Gallen-Kallela's 1896 illustration of the Finnish epic *Kalevala*.

HEROIC JOURNEYS
Quests undertaken by heroes can be reminiscent of shamans' perilous journeys. From Indo-Iranian epics to the Greek *Odyssey* and the Caucasian *Nart Sagas*, illustrated here by Makharbek Tuganov, challenges encountered by heroes may be interpreted as shamanic battles against intangible enemies and forces.

91   FOUNDATIONS — 3 — *Religious (Dis-) Connections*

religions, such as Christianity and Islam, on shamanic societies resulted in the loss or reduction of knowledge associated with their rituals and beliefs. It is, however, possible to see shamanic traces even in places where an imposed new religion has been pervasive.

Several practices associated with mystical Hinduism, for example, reveal traits that have parallels with shamanic ordeals. Such rituals as walking on blades, using hooks to pierce the flesh, or climbing the sacrificial post (*yūpārohaṇa*) suggest links to the techniques that shamans use to prove their exceptional powers and their ability to transcend this reality and ascend to the heavens. Even the elusive drink *soma*, mentioned in the oldest texts of Hinduism, the Vedas, and in the Zoroastrian Avesta, may be linked to intoxicating drinks and substances used by shamans to open the spiritual doors to numinous realms. In India, Chola-period representations of the Hindu god Shiva from the thirteenth century CE show him with datura buds in his headdress; this flower has psychotropic effects when ingested. Perhaps not coincidentally, the proven link between plants, divination, medicine and cure led some communities exposed to Hinduism, such as the Nepalese Tamang, to consider Shiva the patron of healing shamans, and his symbol, the *trishula* ('trident'), appears on their drums. This clearly indicates exchanges between belief systems that, at least in part, seem peacefully to co-exist and inform each other.

In prehistoric China the iconography of funerary art, bronzes and divination kits testifies to the activity of shamans. They appear on Shang-period vessels (eleventh century BCE) alongside their spirit helpers, specifically tigers, who seem to have assisted them in communicating with royal ancestors and spirits.

Visual references to Chinese women shamans (addressed with the term *wu*) appear in later Zhou-dynasty plastic arts (1046–256 BCE), most significantly in figurines of dancers wearing long-sleeved tunics. These floating sleeves were used in swirling motions to help the women enter a trance. They suggest parallels with historical shamans' fringed robes, which

Dancing Dervishes, attributed to Bhizad, Iran, *c.* 1480

Sufism is probably the Islamic sect closest to shamanism, because it includes practices, such as intentional trance states, that pre-date Islam. This miniature from a manuscript of the poems of Hafiz depicts a Sufi ceremony where music is used to hypnotize dancers into a spinning daze, a collective rapture that puts them in contact with the divine.

DECODING TAMANG SHAMANIC DRUM HANDLE

Squeezed between Tibetan Buddhism, Bön and Hinduism, Nepalese shamans (*jhākris*) have historically incorporated external religious and cultural influences into their beliefs and crafts. The handles of their drums (*dhyāngro*) reveal the syncretic extent of Nepalese *jhākris*' shamanism. This particular *dhyāngro* was used by a shaman of the Tamang people. Symbolizing the upper, central and lower worlds through its three sections, the handle's lower part is wedged into the ground during parts of shamanic rituals. Below, a *dhyāngro* can be seen being used by a *jhākri* in East Nepal.

FACES
Nepalese shamanic drum handles regularly feature carvings of faces. These are variably interpreted as the faces of shamanic ancestors, Buddhist guardians or lamas, or as representing the three aspects of Shiva.

1.

VAJRA
Carved into this drum handle is a *vajra*, a Buddhist ritual object that represents thunder. Testament to the influence of Buddhism on Nepalese shamanism is the recurrence of the *vajra* in the *jhākris'* visual culture.

2.

ENDLESS KNOT
Endless knots are often carved into drum handles; here one forms the centre of the *vajra*. In Buddhism, the knot represents the everlasting movement of time and the mind. It is also an auspicious symbol in Hinduism.

3.

RELIGIOUS SYMBOL
Here we see a *trishula* (Shiva's trident) carved into the drum's handle. Other religious symbols that are often featured include *nagas*, sacred snakes for both Hindus and Buddhists, and the cosmic symbol *om*.

4.

PHURBA
The bottom of the handle is carved into the shape of a *phurba*, a ritual dagger that originated in Tibetan Buddhism and Bön. It is considered a sceptre of power that fights evil and stops negative influences.

5.

FOUNDATIONS — 3 — *Religious (Dis-) Connections*

Shin Yun-bok, *The Dance of a Shaman*, c. 18th century
The long, flowing sleeves of Korean shamans' robes evoke birds' wings. Birds have a special relationship with shamans, who are said to be able to fly. Dances reproducing birds' movements may have old shamanic origins.

mimic the birds' feathers that supposedly helped them fly. Interestingly, these Chinese garments have similarities with those of contemporary Korean women shamans called *mudang*, who employ swirling motions in their rituals. Early Chinese shamanism lost its social power after the fifth century BCE; its values were at odds with the new standards being embraced as dynastic power strengthened, strict imperial hierarchies and roles were imposed, and Confucianism was introduced. Shamans were downgraded to simple diviners as geomancy and fortune-telling were consolidated into special roles within the courts.

The situation among nomadic Mongolian peoples was different. The unification of the empire under Chinggis Khan in the first quarter of the thirteenth century CE incorporated shamans within Tengrism, the official religion of the Mongols. Tengrism, often dubbed 'Mongolian shamanism', is heavily based on the animistic principles shared by most herding peoples of Central Asia. It was largely replaced after the adoption of Buddhism, starting from the end of the Mongolian empire around the end of the thirteenth century.

Bön demon, Samye Monastery, 2009
Tibetan Buddhism has variably incorporated Bön deities in its pantheon. Bön has historically been the conduit of shamanic traits in Tibetan religious life.

This resulted in the classic distinction between Yellow shamans, whose work has been inflected by Buddhism and who work with the sky and the heavens, and Black shamans, who resisted external influences and continue to fight evil spirits and demons.

In the traditional Tibetan religion called Bön, there are classes of ritual specialists called *'das log*, who display clear shamanic traits despite obvious references to Buddhist concepts such as post-mortem journeys in the land of the dead. Their travels to the netherworld on behalf of a client are achieved through an induced trance. Other classes of practitioners, called *rnga*, perform their spiritual travels sitting on a drum, appropriately enough given the divinatory function of this object in most parts of the shamanic world. Clearly, shamanic configurations here work in tandem with more structured religious frameworks. For the most part, when Buddhism encountered societies in which shamanic traits were essential elements of the belief system, Buddhists tended to consider them part of a separate religion. But this was not the fate of shamanism under Islam and Christianity.

Árpád Feszty, *Arrival of the Hungarians* (detail), 1892–94

This is a rare image of a Hungarian táltos, a figure equivalent to a shaman. The gender-ambiguous character is depicted overseeing what appears to be a ritual pyre, probably a metaphor for the impending demise of shamanism under Christianized Hungarians.

As in the cases of Hinduism and Bön, Islam's encounter with shamanism resulted in syncretic solutions, whose detectable traits can be mostly identified in the practices of some Islamic sects, as well as Sufi customs and traditions. The Turkish religious sect of the Alevi-Bektashi, who originate from the nomadic Turkmen tribes of Central Asia, retain certain dance moves typical of the shamanic performances of their forebears. Most notable are the ancient crane dances that mimic the flight of this mighty bird, whose shamanic links are undisputed.

In the early phases of Islamization in Central Asia, shamanic practices such as divination and trance resonated with the mystical vein adopted by Sufis. It was this form of Islam into which shamanic traits were most successfully integrated, but with time the shaman (known by the name *bakhshi*) became a mix between a bard, a diviner and a healer. These figures were associated with the stringed instrument called a *kobyz*, which had historically been the preferred

instrument of Turkic shamans from the Karakalpak, Kazakh, Kyrgyz and Tatar peoples, who used it to banish illness and diseases. Interestingly, some of these instruments represent horses, a very important animal in ancient Central Asian shamanism.

Musical instruments remained in use as healing tools in Central Asia throughout the twentieth century, when Uzbek gender-crossing shamans are known to have used drums in their practice. To this day, music is used for this purpose, especially in Uzbekistan and Afghanistan, where stringed instruments are still employed in healing rituals performed in remote areas. Although forms of Islam such as Sufism may have been originally more permeable to pre-existing cultural traits, by and large, the dominant doctrinal view is that shamanism clashes with Islam's precepts, proscriptions and prescriptions. As such, it has been historically banned in officially Islamic territories despite occasionally re-emerging in marginal communities.

< **Saint Stephen of Perm**
Orthodox Eastern Church missionary Stephen of Perm was instrumental in bringing Christianity to remote areas of Asia. Oral traditions tell of a magical battle between this saint and local shamans (tun). It is said that shamans' spells were weaker than prayers and, as a consequence, the duel culminated in the victory of Christianity over shamanism.

> **Paul Drozdowski, Saint Peter the Aleut, 2009**
Unangan Saint Peter the Aleut from Alaska, known as Cungagnaq, converted to Eastern Orthodox Christianity and was eventually killed by Spanish Roman Catholics for refusing to renounce his faith. Aleuts and other Indigenous Alaskan peoples began renouncing shamanism in the 18th century under pressure from Russian missionaries.

Christianity has historically adopted a similar stance towards shamanism, associating it in general with paganism, idolatry and devil worship. This attitude is explicit in the negative judgments that have coloured Christian historiography about shamanism since the Middle Ages. The arrival of Christianity in today's Hungary between the tenth and eleventh centuries marked a decisive shift away from the acceptance of Indigenous beliefs mirrored in the practices of local shamans called *táltos*. Though Hungary has been officially a Christian nation since late antiquity, references to *táltos* appear in Hungarian historiography throughout the eighteenth century, indicating that they were far from forgotten.

As early as the fourteenth century, Orthodox missionaries from Eastern Europe such as Stephen of Perm (1340–1396) successfully stamped out shamanism among the Komi people of Siberia, converting them after destroying their idols.

Further attempts to eliminate shamanism among European peoples took place in Scandinavia among the Indigenous Saami from the seventeenth century. No attempt was made to incorporate Christianity into

< Pelagie Inuk, Canada, 1951
The arrival of Christianity greatly affected Inuit groups living in the Arctic. Shamanism was banned in Christianized territories, and some communities fully embraced the new faith. Sister Pelagie Inuk was the first Inuit nun.

> Alexander Gabyshev, Russia, 2021
Imprisoned for his anti-Putin views, this Yakut shaman is among a long list of shamans historically detained in Russia. Today, former state repression of shamanism has been replaced by political censorship.

the pre-existing beliefs of the Saami, who were banned from following their traditional religion by successive generations of Protestant authorities. Campaigns to eradicate shamanism from Saapmi (the area inhabited by the Saami) targeted the *noaidis* (Saami shamans), partly by burning the drums through which the shamans made their predictions, cured the sick and forecasted the weather. Though nominally Christian, many Saami resisted assimilation and, at least in part, managed to maintain their shamanic beliefs while keeping them hidden from Christians and missionaries.

The situation was no different among the agrarian societies of northern Italy in the sixteenth century. Some shamanic traits have been detected in the *benandanti* ('those that walk well', or 'that walk the right path'). Widely accused by the Catholic Church of consorting with Satan, the *benandanti*, whose crime was to admit to fighting evil forces while in a state of trance, were persecuted for supposed devil worship and witchcraft. Their nightly battles and trances occurred side by side with Catholicism, which – at least in principle – they did not renounce. They found

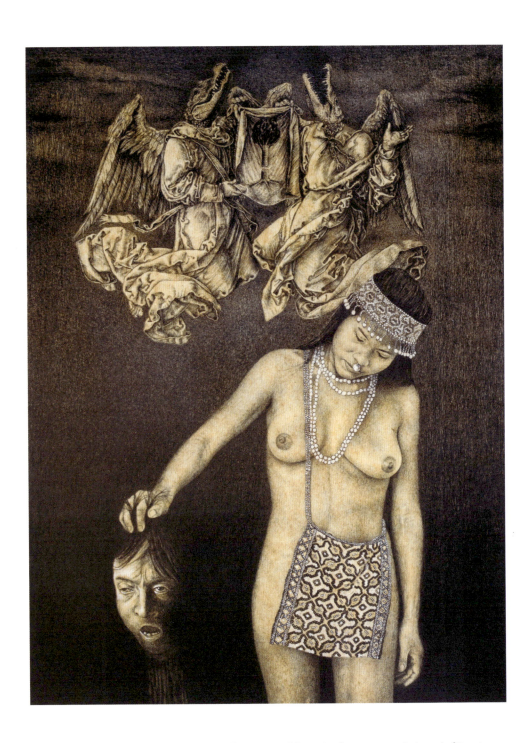

Miguel Vilca Vargas, ***The Temptation of Magdelena Cumapa,*** **2017**

The Catholic imagery and shamanic references present in the work of Peruvian artist Miguel Vilca Vargas reveal the mutual entanglement of precolonial and colonial beliefs in the Amazonian tropics. Shamanism is common among Peruvian mestizos, and among forest peoples such as the Shipibo-Conibo.

FOUNDATIONS —3— *Religious (Dis-)Connections*

no contradiction between Church dictates and their work on behalf of their community.

The impact of Christianity cannot be underestimated among the Native peoples of the Americas. Its presence was often detrimental, yet despite centuries of forced assimilation, conversion efforts and missionary work, shamanism managed to resist and has continued into the twenty-first century in several parts of the continent. The areas first encountered by European colonists, such as the Caribbean islands, experienced the total annihilation of ancient shamanic practices. Catholic missionaries and eyewitnesses described these practices in great detail, before their practitioners almost entirely perished due to epidemics, missions' unsanitary conditions, enslavements and deportations.

Shamanism was also severely disrupted by the arrival of missionaries in the Arctic. They eagerly destroyed shamans' paraphernalia, drums and masks; some survive in ethnographic collections. The Orthodox Eastern Church initiated missionary campaigns in Alaska and the Aleutian Islands from 1794. After the cession of these territories to the USA in 1867, Protestantism began to replace Russian Orthodox Christianity, but the impact on shamanism was equally as disruptive.

Colonial powers banned shamanism, or punished its practitioners, throughout the North American continent, no less so along the Pacific coast of Canada, where the prohibition of traditional ceremonies from 1885 to 1951 severely limited shamanic rituals. Despite vigorous conversion campaigns on both sides of the Canada/USA border, some communities saw in the Christian message interesting parallels with shamanism and integrated some of its ideas and principles into their pre-existing models. Christ, for example, became the master shaman healer. In Christianized Salish communities of the Fraser River, individuals endowed with special abilities, who once would have been considered shamans, turned into healers. Yet the use of ancient instruments such as the drum, and even shamanic rituals such as the

Soul Recovery ceremonies, continued throughout the twentieth century.

In other parts of the Americas, plants once used by northern Mexican shamans, such as the peyote cactus and mescal beans, were also adopted by practitioners of entirely new religions based on Christian precepts. In the nineteenth century a new religion called Native American Church turned the ingestion of the peyote cactus into an Indigenous form of Eucharist. In the USA today, it is the only context in which peyote can be consumed legally.

Similar syncretisms happened in parts of the Americas where Catholicism has been prominent since the sixteenth century, although isolated populations of the tropics may have retained a stronger hold on traditional shamanic practices. The appropriation of crosses, the use of the Bible in ritual, and belief in the intercessions of saints in shamanic ceremonies are common among the Huichol of Mexico and the Chilean Mapuche, although missionaries recognized from the outset that Indigenous believers used only parts of the Christian imagery, doctrine and tenets in order to appear converted.

Institutional religions may have offered new languages in which to reinterpret old ideas and concepts. The degree to which these permitted shamans to remain autonomous entities within the constraints of organized clerical structures varied greatly across time and space. Central religious figures such as Christ or the Buddha may have been locally turned into powerful masters of animals, mighty shamans, healers, deities or culture-heroes. Imported symbols may have merged with old ones, and prerogatives such as cure, divination, fortune-telling, spirit journeys and communication with ancestors or other intangible entities may have become marginal to the official liturgies of dominant faiths. Notwithstanding these changes, shamans have made their presence felt throughout history. In some cases, they radically reformulated both conceptual and formal aspects of new belief systems crystallized in major world religions' precepts and rituals.

> *pages 106–107*
Lu Nan, shamanic seance, 1997
Himalayan shamans usually wear a ringa, a five-pointed crown representing the five aspects of Buddha and other elements of Tibetan Buddhist cosmology. The crown is decorated with white scarves to greet and honour deities taking part in the ritual.

Marian Wesley Smith, Mrs Seymour and her drum, British Columbia, Canada, 1946

Salish peoples' shamanic practices were heavily reinterpreted as the result of Christian missionary work. Both female and male Salish shamans used drums, such as the one pictured, to accompany healing singing sessions. Despite this, old beliefs still retain their persuasive power, yet adopt meanings more suitable to the new religious regimes.

FOUNDATIONS — 3 — *Religious (Dis-) Connections*

THE INTANGIBLE

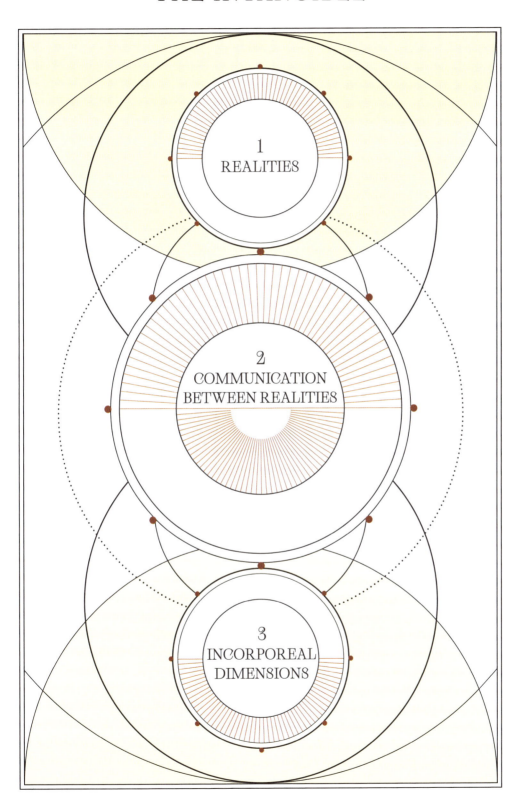

THE INTANGIBLE

REALITIES

'The shamans are swinging a gold net, they put a gold net over the housefront. They drag a gold net as far as the sky. If Muu saw any road through the sky lying open the shamans would rise and would strike with their sticks, and hold their sticks in a line.'

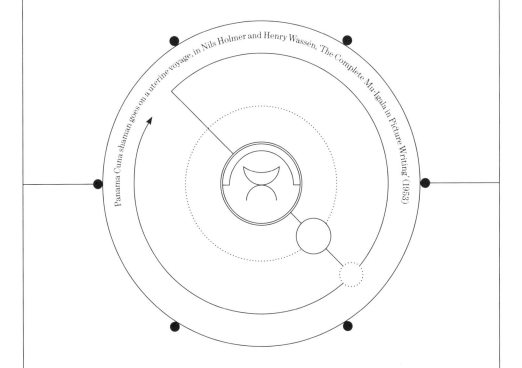

Panama Cuna shaman goes on a uterine voyage, in Nils Holmer and Henry Wassén, 'The Complete Mu-Igala in Picture Writing' (1953)

Seeing and perceiving the world through a shaman's eyes entails suspending judgment about the world of the senses. Shamanic worlds are composed of complex interconnections between perceivable features and invisible essences that only shamans can access. Realities appear to those who can see beyond the visible, a trait that is detectable in shamanic art from around the world, which can be at once deceiving, kaleidoscopic, intricate, paradoxical and baffling.

Whhen Europeans first met shamans in places such as the Americas and Siberia, they immediately dismissed their practices as simple tricks or deceptions with no real legitimacy or validity. Shamans' claims that they could travel in spirit, fight demons or cause storms were discounted as mere fantasies. For the missionaries and Enlightenment travellers who left us precious accounts of shamanic work, rituals and ceremonies, nothing of what these specialists of the intangible did was acceptable, neither on religious nor on scientific grounds. European theological and rational superiority, these travellers reasoned, was sufficiently self-evident to withstand any comparison with the disingenuous performances of misguided conjurers. Even some more recent thinkers from the twentieth century have questioned the soundness of shamans' knowledge and techniques, revealing a fundamental distrust of what (they believed) cogent thinking and deduction could expose as mere mental delusions or prestidigitators' illusions.

Aside from the moral disapproval of the Christian clergy and missionaries, there has been a certain cynicism stemming from a secular conception of the world. In this view, there is no room for the unexplained – which, by contrast, is at the core of shamanic thinking.

The conventional distinction between religion and science (commonly separated into what we believe and what we know) seems to encapsulate the ongoing tension between animistic models of the world, embraced by shamans, and scientific approaches. Though periodic revisions and revaluations, based on new discoveries, are fundamental to the scientific method, at the most elementary level science tends to support the notion of a physical world that is measurable and translatable into models, and can be reduced to mathematical calculations and immutable laws. Today, most people (probably) perceive this inherently universalizing view as an effective and objective way to explain the reality we live in, one that can make sense of almost everything that exists through experimentation and testing.

< *page 108*
Petroglyphs at Chumash Painted Cave State Historic Park, Santa Barbara, California, pre-1700
Displaying a rich iconography of sunbursts, stars, lines, insects and geometric motifs, this cave likely served as a station for shamanic activities, possibly as a place of seclusion during vision quests to contact invisible realms.

< *page 110*
Shipibo-Conibo textile, Iquitos, Peru
Known as Kene, this type of design has its origins in shamanic dreaming. It may cover pots, textiles and other objects. Today this style has become the ethnic signature of groups such as the Shipibo-Conibo of the Peruvian Amazon.

Illustration from Joseph-François Lafitau's *Mœurs des Sauvages Americains, Comparées aux Mœurs des Premiers Temps* **(1724)**

This scene depicts the dream or vision of a group of shamans as a winged figure that resembles a Christian devil. Missionaries, including Lafitau, translated what they witnessed in places such as the Caribbean into concepts from Christian theology. This resulted in the demonization of shamanic practices.

Huichol yarn painting, Mexico

Inspired by visions experienced under the effect of peyote, these types of paintings usually depict conventional themes and motifs, such as dancing shamans, deer, the sun and peyote itself.

Shamans, by and large, adopt an alternative view. They live in a numinous and mysterious world, filled with supernatural risks and dangers, and share a reality with unpredictable beings whose actions may negatively affect human life on this plane of existence. From an animistic perspective, not everything can be known, and certain dimensions of reality should not be disturbed. Interactions with them should be handled only by specialists who wield the power to deal with the unknown.

To shamans, reality is not just what can be seen and explained through logical reasoning, but consists of everything that is experienced by humans, whether understandable or not, whether material or incorporeal. It includes a panoply of possibilities ranging from dreams and visions to apparitions, extrasensory perceptions and near-death and out-of-body experiences, among others. The fact that all humans can potentially experience any of these is taken as proof that reality runs on a continuum, on which all the various levels of the universe bleed into one another.

Homayun Sidky, shaman and patient, Nepal
Spirits may have negative effects on humans, such as causing illness and disease. Shamans' negotiation with spirits is essential for an afflicted person to regain their health.

In the world of the five senses in which animists live, the boundaries that keep reality's dimensions separate are fundamentally porous and permeable and therefore they can be crossed. While ordinary humans may find it difficult to transition between one metaphysical layer and another, intangible other-than-humans can do it more easily. This explains why so many people see undefinable beings, hear strange sounds or disembodied voices, or feel they have been touched or even possessed by incorporeal entities in the phenomenal world. Shamans and their followers' encounters with any of the other-than-humans that inhabit these layers is intimately subjective. In an animistic framework there can be no objective view of the world, because of the instability of the relationship between the physical and the metaphysical; and that relationship must be constantly monitored and managed by competent specialists, namely shamans.

Usually, shamans are more preoccupied with what is lesser known and difficult to explain than with what can be experienced in ordinary life. For shamans, controlling and managing moments of crisis,

DECODING A COLOMBIAN TUKANO VISIONARY DRAWING

This depiction of a vision features many elements that reflect stories of creation, as told by the oral traditions of the Tukano people. Collected by anthropologist Gerardo Reichel-Dolmatoff, who claims it was drawn by Yebá, a Tukano person from the Vaupés area of Colombia, this image is composed of geometric and anthropomorphic motifs. While geometric shapes may be part of a shared

1.

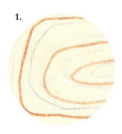

U SHAPE
The sideways U shape represents a door or portal that connects different worlds. Cosmic doors can be physical features or invisible ones that shamans know how to access.

4.

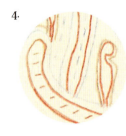

CELESTIAL CANO
The canoe carries so the first humans. Cel canoes are a commo theme in Amazonia accounts, though th are sometimes talke about metaphorical as anacondas.

2.

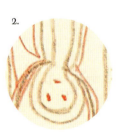

INVERTED HUMAN
This diving person is linked by a meandering line to the canoe, which suggests that the figure is associated with the people in it. He is likely a character from the cycle of accounts that form the creation myth.

5.

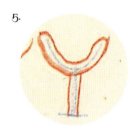

Y SHAPES
This is the shape of a holder, used by Tuka and other Amazonia peoples to rest the r up tobacco they sm Some holders may b enough to reach fro ground to the mout sitting shaman.

3.

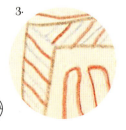

RATTLES AND SONGS
Reichel-Dolmatoff reports that the L shapes are rattles (the shaman's preferred instrument), and the wavy lines depict songs, which can connect humans to the invisible world and transmit knowledge.

6.

SEVEN COLUMN
The seven columns lower part of the im represent songs tha relate to different r of creation. Differe in the designs may for differences in th contents of the myt

116   THE INTANGIBLE —1— *Realities*

visual language across the world, the meanings assigned to each visual element are determined by culture. As such, the motifs here would not make sense without the expert's explanation, which Reichel-Dolmatoff provided in the book in which the image was published, *Beyond the Milky Way: Hallucinatory Imagery of the Tukano Indians* (1978).

Antony Galbraith, *Sedna*, 2015
Inuit shamans frequently contact the powerful being Sedna to persuade her to release the shoals of fish and marine mammals trapped in her long hair.

the unexpected or the unfamiliar is probably more urgent and concerning than anything that everyone can test for themselves – for example, the passing of the seasons, or the maturation of the human body. Although there are classes of specialists who deal directly with these areas of human experience, shamans mostly address exceptional events that may affect everyday life beyond the predictable regularity of its cyclical rhythms. The greater part of shamanic expertise revolves around predicting and interpreting the inscrutable, unfathomable dynamics of the transcendent: the oddities, the exceptions and the inexplicable occurrences.

From a shamanic perspective, dreams and visions are proof that incorporeal realities exist beyond the five senses. These realities may be the realms of the dead and ancestors, who may cause accidents; the worlds of demons and sorcerers, which are the origin of illnesses; and the rarefied realities of animal doubles and their masters. Masters of animals manage the prey flows, or shoals of fish, and may withhold prey from hunters, who often need shamans' mediation to ensure

 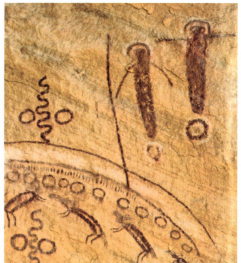

< **Petroglyphs at White Shaman Cave, Val Verde County, Texas, 2500 BCE– 500 CE**
The anthropomorphs depicted in this cave have elongated bodies, possibly a visual representation of the bodily sensations experienced under the effect of mescal beans or peyote.

> **Petroglyphs at Barrier Canyon, Utah, 4000– 1500 BCE**
Realities accessed by shamans are frequently visually reproduced as accounts of extraordinary experiences. Difficult to interpret, these images are depictions of shamans' intimate contact with the intangible.

successful hunting or fishing expeditions. An example is Sedna, mistress of the sea; in Inuit belief, her hair traps the fish needed by humans for their sustenance.

Numerous visual records exist of these parallel realities experienced by shamans. They appear as rock art, etched on bark, painted on vases and represented on textiles. Whether made by shamans or reproduced by independent artists under shamanic supervision, these visual depictions are windows into ways of thinking and experiencing reality that often escape the modern mind. Intricate meanders, figures merging into one another or dazzling motifs present the outside observer with captivating visuals that reflect what reality looks like for shamans and their followers.

It can be difficult for onlookers to make sense of the imagery produced in shamanic contexts, even if they recognize some familiar elements. Contemporary people with materialistic, secular, scientific or technologically oriented minds are mostly used to what is tangible and concrete, and consign the realms of dreams and visions to the dimension of illusion or fantasy. Focus and concentration are required to see through these images, and that is entirely intentional on the part of the makers. Only by carefully examining these representations' complex intertwining of multiple

DECODING TAÍNO SACRED GEOGRAPHY

Many shamanic societies conceptualize their universe as a series of stacked layers. Only shamans are able to travel through these layers during their seances and spirit journeys. An exemplary model of this cosmology is the sacred geography of the Taíno peoples of the Antilles, who were encountered by Christopher

UPPER WORLD

Taíno sacred geography placed sky beings in the upper world. These beings were birds, such as owls or woodpeckers and bats. Owls were associated with the spirits of the night, and bats and woodpeckers also had significant roles in Taíno mythology.

1.

MIDDLE WORLD

Humans and animals inhabited the middle layer. Though non-shamans couldn't travel beyond this plane, caves were a point of access to the lower world. Caves were decorated with shamanic animals and motifs and used for ancestor worship ceremonies.

4.

COSMIC PILLAR

The notion of a celestial vault supported by a cosmic pillar is not uncommon. Among the Taíno, the pillar was conceptualized as a giant tree with branches that kept the sky in place and a trunk that reached the underworld to hold the universe together.

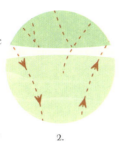

2.

INTER-WORLD TRAVEL

The Taíno had a complex cosmology in which shamans had a central role. Their work required them to travel between the three cosmic tiers to manage a web of relationships between the living, the dead and other-than-human beings.

5.

BALLCOURT

Ballcourts, the setting for ceremonial ball games, were the focus of Taíno social life and were conceived of as the centre of the world. They served as the burial site for ancestors, whose effigies were often carved on the flat stone slabs that surrounded the arena.

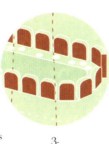

3.

LOWER WORLD

This realm was inhabited by ancestors and water beings. Waterfowl and amphibians were especially important because their access to water and land made them mediators between worlds. Manatees, neither fish nor terrestrial animals, may have also belonged to this category.

6.

Columbus and described by father Ramón Pané, the first eradicator of Indigenous beliefs in the Americas. Though cosmological maps may resemble each other in many parts of the world, the idea that their regions are connected and that only some people can travel through them is distinctive of shamanic societies.

Norval Morrisseau, panels four and six from *Man Changing into Thunderbird*, 1977
For Canadian Anishinaabe people, shape-shifting is a fact of life. However, only powerful shamans can turn into powerful beings, such as the mighty Thunderbird.

figures is it possible to detect singular characters, or parts of their bodies, as they emerge from kaleidoscopic backgrounds. This visual strategy clearly denotes a world in which certain dimensions only appear if one can truly 'see'. Shamans are very much aware of the deceiving nature of outward appearances, as humans, animals and other beings may not be what they look like at first sight.

It is not coincidence to find intricate designs that express such views in cultural contexts in which shamanism is the dominant model for interacting with different layers of a multiplanar cosmos. Textiles from the Pacific Northwest Coast of North America, ceramics from the prehistoric Amazon, pottery from pre-Columbian Panama and contemporary Mexican Huichol yarn paintings are all examples of this way of visualizing the dynamic interaction of different planes of reality. Several registers are experienced at once as the shaman seamlessly moves between them. To an external viewer, these elaborate motifs may appear confusing and abstract, but to the shamanic mind they present a very real, and yet conceptual, image of the interdependence between the seen and the unseen. Though some of these artefacts may not have been made by shamans themselves, they reflect a permeating and shared approach to what is real between the materiality of the world and the immateriality of the transcendent.

Local artists devised different solutions to express the unfamiliar, dynamic and perplexing states accessible through shamanic practice. They played with cognition through visual deception, optical illusions, indeterminacy, ambiguity and the oversaturation of the decorated surface (i.e. *horror vacui*, or fear of empty space), among other visual techniques. Each of these forms plays with different types of observers' perceptions, and the multiple cognitive and perceptual states experienced in a shamanic lifeworld.

In all these expressions, beings that emerge from one another are as much part of their background as the background is generated by them: a paradox that can only make sense for those who have developed a shamanic way of seeing.

Paradox is part of reality. We are often asked to believe in the existence of things we cannot see and this is perhaps the only point of convergence between science and shamanism. Even scientists agree that there is much that science cannot explain and, what is

< Pedestal bowl with anthropomorphic reptile, Coclé culture, Panama, 1100–1300 CE
This bowl may depict a transforming shaman surrounded by supernatural power. The lines of energy (or stingray spines) that surround the body are associated with the shamanic iconography of this region.

> Pedestal bowl with sea monster, Coclé culture, Panama, 1000–1100 CE
The sea monster's sinuous movements create intricate overlaps of different visual planes, which represent the multilayered universe inhabited by Panamanian shamans.

DECODING CHILKAT BLANKET

Pacific Northwest cultures produced dazzling images of the shamanic worldview. This one is Tlingit, from the late 1800s. The complexity of Chilkat-style imagery has baffled art historians and anthropologists for centuries: its composite figures do not resemble anything visible in the corporeal world, and their layered composition makes it difficult to distinguish where one being ends and another begins. This visual strategy reflects philosophies related to the nature of reality and the interconnectedness of all beings, visible and invisible.

SPLIT REPRESENTATION
The notion of split representation refers to the symmetrical relationship between two halves of the visual field along the central axis. The central character is built by aligning two profiles, joining at the centre, to create a full figure.

CENTRAL FIGURE
Chilkat blankets usually have a central figure surrounded by complementary elements. It is difficult to establish with certainty what these figures represent, but here it appears to be a Thunderbird, identifiable by its wings and talons.

LAYERED COMPOSITION
Chilkat artists build their images so that elements appear and disappear when one focuses on the foreground or background. This signifies that the universe is made of multiple layers and that humans can't always make sense of its nature.

FACES
When portrayed separately from a human body, the face becomes a symbol that marks any being as having intentionality and the ability to affect the world through its actions. A face can therefore signify a human or a human-like being.

SIMULTANEITY
Here a human face and a bear are visible at once as themselves and as part of other bodies; the images are simultaneously themselves and others. Figures are represented at once as what humans know and what they reveal themselves to be.

INDIVIDUAL ELEMENTS
Pacific Northwest styles are made up of primary, secondary and tertiary elements, including stylized details from the natural world – such as eyes, fins, ears, claws, teeth, beaks and feathers – that are variably combined to form complex configurations.

Figure of a shaman prepared for burial, attributed to Sdiihldaa/Simeon Stilthda, Haida culture, Pacific Northwest, 19th century
The shaman is represented wearing his ceremonial fringed apron. The Haida believed in reincarnation, which was usually announced by dreams or omens. Shamans' corpses were placed away from the village due to the risk posed by their power.

more, that a fair amount of belief is needed to accept the reality of certain facts. In the realm of quantum physics, for example, no one has ever seen the Higgs boson with their own eyes, but science tells us it exists.

Scientists reach their conclusions based on logic, process of elimination, rigorous trial and error, and investigation of cause and effect. Yet, as shamans would have it, not all causal relations can be explained through the scientific method. In fact, rather than testing the world to uncover the inherent laws of the universe, shamans adopt an open-ended attitude to facts and events, especially those that cannot be easily explained. For shamans, the real testing grounds are the subterranean realms of the universe where the laws of physics do not apply. In fact, often the laws are the very opposite of those on Earth: the inversion of social norms is described in shamans' oral accounts of the worlds they experience. Equally, as many experts maintain, we can appreciate the visualizations of the intangible realities visited by shamans through the images they left in rock art and other expressive forms. Such images depict things that are in direct contrast to what a scientific view of the world finds acceptable: namely that humans can fly, or can see through somebody's skin, or merge into plants. These themes appear in shamanic images produced over the millennia.

The notion of second sight, associated with all shamans, is visualized in multifarious forms across

Textile fragment, Paracas culture, Peru, 450–175 BCE
This is the conventional pose for a flying shaman in Paracas. This may be a visual metaphor for the individual's spirit journey or a representation of a shaman's ability to fly.

different cultures. So-called X-ray vision, or the ability to see a human's insides, is variably expressed by the depiction of rib cages, skulls or internal organs on sculptures, clothing and, more recently, on paper. Shamans are said to use this skill to cure and heal, and to find the sources of illness, usually by linking what they see in the body to its supernatural origins.

The complex iconographies painted, scratched or etched on cave walls and boulders may be understood through careful decoding and interpretation. Though this is not universally accepted, rock art scholars argue that such shamanistic interpretations may have some factual basis, especially in areas where shamans' use of entheogens (psychoactive substances) and trance are a matter of record. Regions such as southern Texas and northern Mexico, Baja California, several parts of the Amazonian basin, Central Asia, Siberia and southern Africa are usually listed among the places where historical populations demonstrate a substantial cultural continuity with prehistoric societies. Rock art's visualizations of parallel realities are sometimes rendered in full colour. They are composed into exuberant scenes of transformation, spiritual battles and encounters with other-than-human beings.

Some of the scenes depicted in rock art have been interpreted as metaphors of death and resurrection. More specifically, powerful representations of people drowning are seen to depict the temporary condition experienced by shamans while in a trance. Various scenes appear to document visually other sensations belonging to altered states of mind, such as energy discharges from the head, tingling produced by a feeling of insects crawling under the skin, the perception of limbs stretching, and even the experience of being dismembered. Shamans discuss these experiences as real and not – as scientists would state – as the result of the ingestion of psychotropic agents, or the effect of sensory deprivation, lack of sleep, meditation, rhythmic drumming or fasting.

According to shamans, these images are not solely renderings of what is seen, but also depictions of what can be experienced. This includes sensations and multisensory perceptions that can only be translated into visual forms by making parallels with situations derived from the world of the five senses. So, for example, images of figures flying are rather common, because of the sensation of being lifted into the air that may happen in dreams, and the sense of lightness that comes from leaving one's body reported by many who have gone through near-death experiences. Some shamans claim to be able to teleport themselves to distant places, offering proof by describing unknown sites in great detail.

Observers outside shamanism may not be convinced by shamans' claims and explanations because those claims contradict all they know about reality, and all the principles of the unchangeable laws to which they are accustomed. Shamans, on the other hand, live and experience realities in which what is out of the ordinary is an integral part of everyday life and cannot be dismissed as illusion. Shamanic lifeworlds operate under different premises: notably, that the unknown, inexplicable and unreachable recesses of the metaphysical world exist, and that despite being elusive and ungraspable by most people, they can be accessed, experienced and described by individuals endowed with special powers.

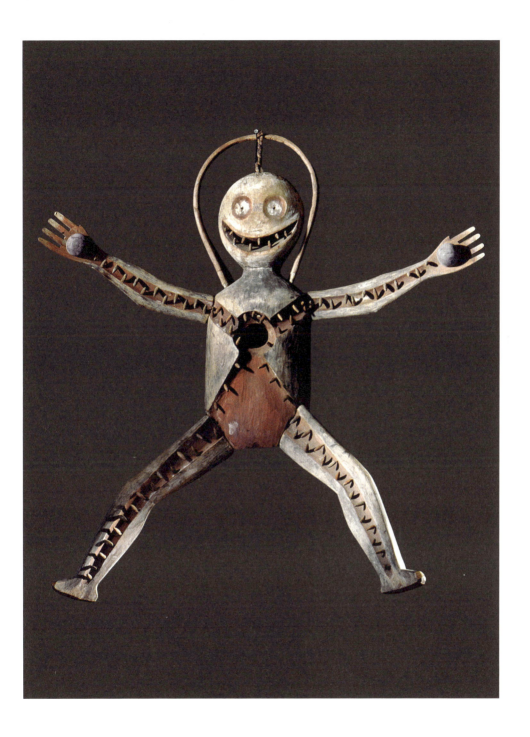

Wooden mask, Alaska, *c.* **1860–80** *This mask shows a splayed anthropomorph split open to display his innards. Such representations reference shamans' ability to see through the skin to diagnose illness and disease. Skeletons, skulls and rib cages are common in shamanic iconography across the world.*

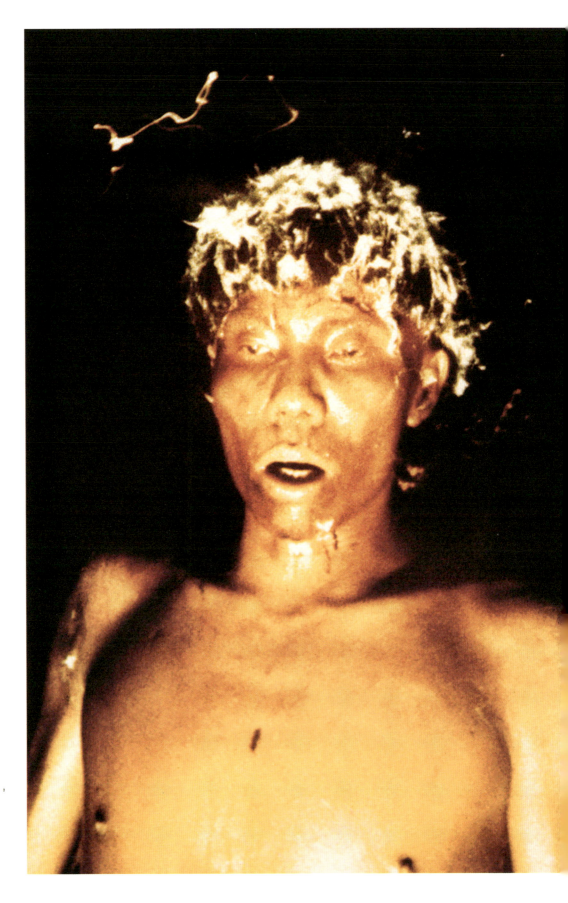

COMMUNICATION BETWEEN REALITIES

'The shamans are held in great esteem by the people;
they pretend to correspond with the shaytan, or devil;
by whom, they say, they are informed of all past and
future events, at any distance of time or place.'

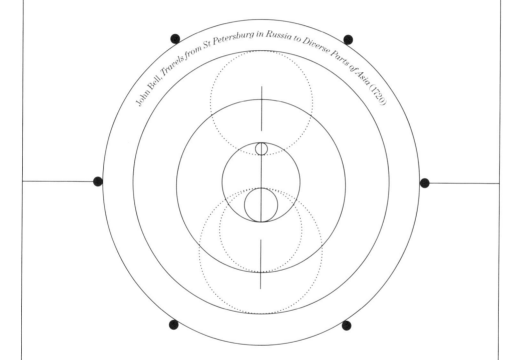

John Bell, *Travels from St Petersburg in Russia to Diverse Parts of Asia* (1720)

Out-of-body experiences occur across the world, yet despite
apparent similarities, they are substantially different in intensity,
purpose and cultural content. Uniquely, shamanic trances are managed
by practitioners who can separate their souls from their bodies to journey
into the cosmos and gain knowledge. The deliberate decision to go into a
trance is what makes shamanic experiences stand out from the various
spontaneous experiences of mystics, saints, prophets and oracles.

Tucked away in a side chapel of the church of Santa Maria della Vittoria in Rome, Italy, there is a marble statue of St Teresa of Avila (1515–1582), the Spanish nun known for her intense spiritual encounters with the divine. The sculptor portrays her in a state of rapture, her head tilted back, as she succumbs to the power of an incoming arrow directed towards her chest, an experience that she vividly describes in her diaries. Entitled *The Ecstasy of Saint Teresa*, the sculpture captures a non-ordinary experience during which common reality and normal senses are temporarily suspended. Persons undergoing such an experience engage with a different state, separate from everyday life, in which their consciousness tunes into metaphysical dimensions. Trance, possession, rapture and swoon are alternative terms for such extraordinary episodes; today, all these are encompassed by the description Alternative (or Adjusted) State of Consciousness (ASC), a neutral definition that stresses the equal validity of different states of consciousness.

Often, these events are associated with religion or spirituality because they deal with transcendent and metaphysical aspects of human life. Saints, mystics and even ordinary people from many religious persuasions have described similar experiences in very evocative terms, using the language of religion, both in personal accounts and in hagiographies. Trances, ecstasies and ASCs are also known from historical texts, ethnographic descriptions, travel literature and eyewitness accounts. Within orthodox Sunni Islam, followers of the mystic Bektashi order of the Sufi have been known to withstand intense scarification procedures while in a state of mystical rapture. Similarly exceptional are the semi-conscious states attained by Hindu devotees of the god Murugan in order to perform the annual ritual of Kavadi Aattam. In this endurance sacrifice, the bodies of male worshippers are pierced by dozens of sharp skewers fixed on semicircular structures carried on the shoulders.

Many such occurrences have been recorded from around the world, and parallels between Sufi fakirs, Christian hermits, Muslim ascetics, Indian yogis,

⟨ *page 130*
Claudia Andujar, 'Collective take of the yãkoana hallucinogen, Catrimani', from the series *O reabu*, 1972–76
Yãkoana is the pulverized resin from trees of the Virola family. It is ingested to summon the masters of nature called xapiripë. Indigenous American shamans' botanical knowledge is demonstrated by their extensive use of a variety of seeds, leaves, vines, cactuses and flowers, as well as gums and resins.

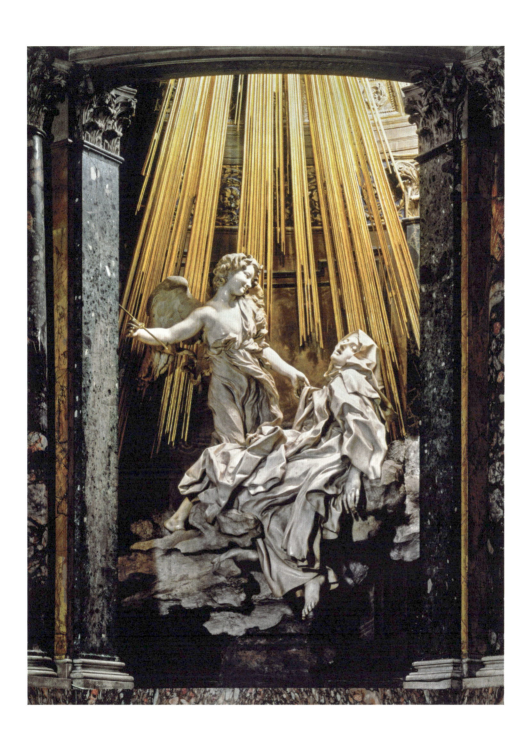

Gian Lorenzo Bernini, *Ecstasy of Saint Teresa*, Rome, 1647–52

This scene is a visualization of an episode described in Saint Teresa of Avila's diaries. Mystical encounters with the divine, such as those of Christian saints, differ from shamanic trances because they are underpinned by the belief in the existence of a free soul that leaves the body to travel to other worlds.

PROFILE
BEHAVIOURS
OF ASC

What are today known as ASCs have been reported in ancient and modern societies worldwide, yet debate over the various forms of ASC is ongoing. Behaviours of people in ASCs may include catatonic stillness, voice changes, contortions and even violent reactions. Often, such experiences are interpreted as the opening of portals to invisible worlds. On the left, Russell Lee's 1946 image shows snake handling in a Pentecostal church in Kentucky, a rite that can involve spirit possession.

ECSTASY
The word ecstasy has been used to describe experiences of union with God: Christian mystics, such as Saint Francis, Hildegard von Bingen and Hadewych, Sufi saints and Jewish prophets are said to have had such encounters.

FRENZIED RAPTURE
Derived from Greek, the original definition of enthusiasm meant 'inspired or possessed by a god'. It was applied to the frenzied raptures experienced by early Christian mystics and, famously, the Greek followers of Dionysus.

SPIRIT POSSESSION
Spirits can be erratic and evil. When they possess someone, they take control and speak through them. Spirit possession is central to some Asian cultures and several African and Afro-American religions, such as Voodooism and Candomblé.

TRANCE
Trance is a state in which a person following specific techniques removes themselves from ordinary life. Mediums go into a trance when they contact spirits that send messages only intelligible to the consultation's sponsors.

MEDITATION
The deep state of focused concentration achieved by yogis, Buddhist monks and ascetics through tranquillity, meditation is a form of disconnection from mundane activities and is aimed at spiritual contemplation.

SHAMANIC JOURNEY
Contrary to spirit possession, where the body is temporarily inhabited by external entities, shamans deliberately leave their body in incorporeal form to make journeys accompanied by their tutelary guides.

THE INTANGIBLE — 2 — *Communication Between Realities*

Devotee of the Hindu god Murugan, Singapore, 2013
Worshippers of Murugan pledge to mortify their flesh in honour of their god. The altered state they experience helps them to face the pain.

and shamans, among others, suggest commonalities that seem to originate in human brain structure, cognitive systems and neuro-physiology. In the past, some psychoanalysts concluded that shamans who entered such extraordinary states were psychologically anomalous individuals, arguing that this was proved by the relatively low number of cases reported in human history. Yet, on purely statistical grounds, the high incidence of this phenomenon among shamans does not support this thesis. There is no evidence that in shamanic contexts allegedly mentally ill people automatically become shamans. In fact, individual shamans may lead very ordinary lives, showing no sign of psychological or mental problems.

Though psychology, psychoanalysis and cognitive sciences may offer some insights into the mental processes involved in such events, they cannot explain the frequency with which ecstasies, out-of-body experiences, trances or dissociative conditions and ASCs occur in both shamanic and other contexts. Religious studies and anthropological research suggest that these episodes may be different in shamanic and

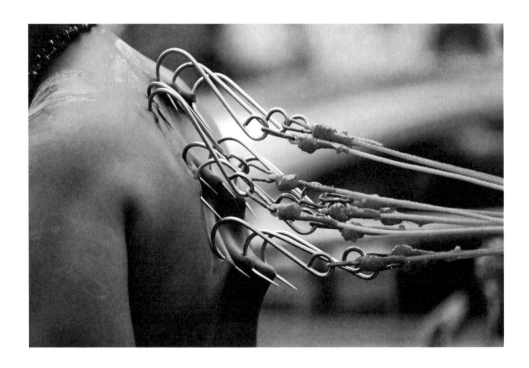

Fakir, India, c. 1890
Sufi ascetics, such as fakirs, use physical techniques to reach Alternative States of Consciousness.

Coptic Christian hermit, Lalibela, Ethiopia
Isolation in caves allows hermits of every religion to reach deep states of concentration, which enables them to achieve some degree of connection to the divine.

non-shamanic contexts. Among shamans, they are the result of years of training, the use of particular methods to attain concentration, and special physical and mental techniques variously developed in different parts of the world for different aims. Socio-religious and cultural patterns not only account for the extreme variation of practices employed by shamans to reach an ASC, but also expose the different nature of these practitioners' experiences in ways that defy simple comparisons.

It is very difficult to establish universal parameters for evaluating how shamanic trances or ecstasies differ from other ASCs. Such evaluations depend not only on the partial, biased and often superficial descriptions collected over time, but also on the use of specific terminologies that have greatly skewed our current understanding of the processes that shamans follow to tune into and communicate with metaphysical realms.

Though today entirely dismissed as derogatory, inaccurate and discriminatory, labels such as 'hysterical', 'schizophrenic', 'delusional', 'neurotic' and 'downright crazy' have been applied to shamans since the beginnings of European interest in the subject. These terms recast what is now called ASC into the

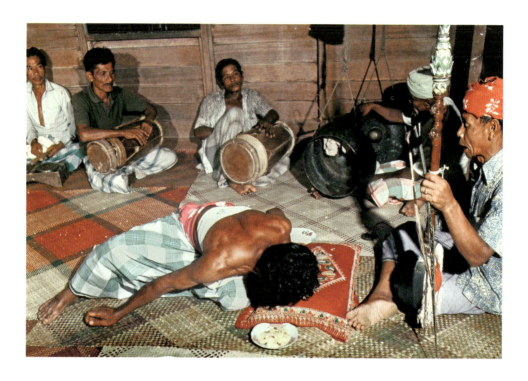

Luca Tettoni, folk medicine practitioner, Bomoh, Malaysia, 2009
South East Asian healers use trance to diagnose the cause of disease. Possessions by spirits or ancestors are difficult to distinguish from shamanic soul travels.

realm of mental illness, limiting shamans' experiences to what happens in their (supposedly disordered) minds. These pejorative definitions appeared and disappeared with the ebbs and flows of Western scientific discourse, and the epochal thrusts driven by medicine, psychoanalysis and even natural sciences. At the end of the nineteenth and the beginning of the twentieth centuries some Westerners mistakenly believed that a condition called 'Arctic hysteria' was at the origin of shamans' visions. It was said to be triggered by the harsh conditions experienced by peoples living in boreal regions of North America, Greenland and Asia.

Between the 1960s and 1970s, both studies in social science and popular discourses on shamanism were dominated by research on psychedelics, and so-called shamanic 'visionary' experiences were discussed in terms of hallucinations and altered states, bringing shamans close to those who experimented with different types of drugs in the cosmopolitan West. In Russia, by contrast, Soviet-era scientists explored the interface between brainwaves, brain chemistry and

Roger Bamber, shaman healing a patient, Sussex, England, 2006
Western healing practices often incorporate shamanic techniques, such as drumming, aimed at soul retrieval or spirit healing.

the meditative states produced by rhythmic drumming in their studies of shamans' changed mental states. Today, elements of these findings have filtered through into the thinking of Neo-Shamans and followers of New Age-style healing, who claim that drumming, humming and other vibrations have a positive effect on recovery from mental and psychological disorders.

Altogether, the focus of much of this research has been on the physiological and metabolic effects of shamanic techniques on the human mind and brain. Little research has been done to link shamans' methods to the different realities they access during the sessions in which they appear to leave the corporeal plane and travel outside the body. This may be partially due to the difficulties in reproducing suitable conditions in scientific laboratories, but also because not all the recorded examples of communication between realities entertained by shamans may describe the same phenomena; and what is more, channels for communicating between physical and metaphysical planes may be used for entirely different purposes.

The all-embracing descriptor ASC, applied to shamanic extraordinary states, encompasses a multiplicity of cases. The use of the plural indicates that there may be variations of degree, if not differences in the nature of these events. Deep meditation, for example, enables Buddhists or yogis to detach themselves from ordinary reality. Tibetan oracles willingly activate an adjusted state in which they become open to receiving into their bodies spirit entities, who will deliver messages from the beyond using the host's voice. Most scholars today would claim that these instances are substantially different from a shamanic journey to other realms. Shamanic journeying requires different techniques, though the resulting changes in perception and mental state are outwardly similar to those of other practitioners.

During a seance, shamans show all the signs of not being their ordinary selves, and this has encouraged some people to see similarities between shamanic experience and rapture, dissociation, possession and trance. Shamans say that they temporarily leave their body in spirit, existing only in immaterial form in metaphysical planes. Descriptions of shamans in this state vary, but many accounts stress how they collapse, unresponsive, after exerting themselves in what appear to be strenuous fights and efforts, which may include heavy breathing, screaming, shrieking and jumping to avoid obstacles and fatal blows struck by malignant forces. Not all seances are the same, as each one is meant to achieve something different. Shamans may need to consult their guides and learn from them. Peruvian *mestizo* shamans ingest a psychoactive beverage called ayahuasca in order to receive knowledge about the world, disease and witchcraft, but such sessions can be used for entirely different purposes. Inuit shamans prefer to fight their opponents on the immaterial plane and do this in a trance state. Kichwa shamans from Ecuador use their ASC to neutralize aggressors' powers, and shamans of the Siberian Evenk, Dolgan and Nganasan turn the seance into an opportunity to talk to the masters of animals. Speaking to the lords of the underworld

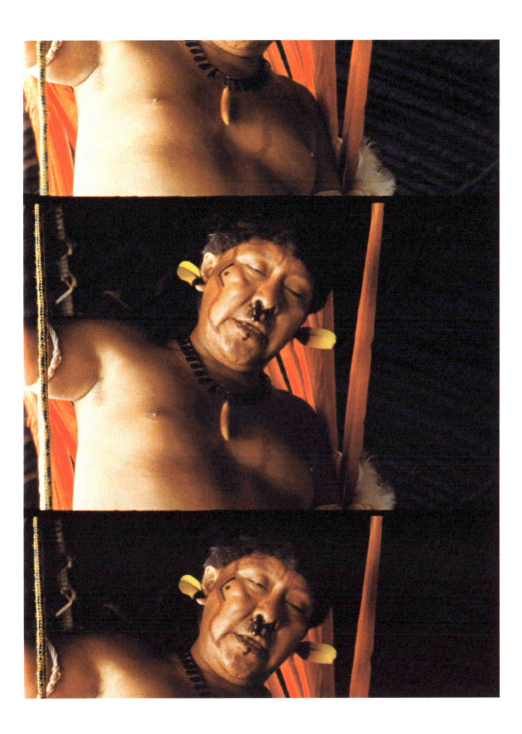

Raymond Depardon, Yanomami man, Brazil, 2002

This man is shown experiencing an Alternative (or Adjusted) State of Consciousness. Messages received during a seance need to be carefully interpreted by shamans. ASCs do not prevent interaction with the world of the five senses; shamans' work entails a degree of awareness of what is happening around them during their seance.

141   THE INTANGIBLE — 2 — *Communication Between Realities*

Pablo Amaringo, *Misterio Profundo* ('Deep Mystery'), 2012

According to Peruvian artist Pablo Amaringo, this painting represents the wisdom of plants and how they help shamans to gain deeper knowledge and understanding of life's mysteries. Inspired by visions resulting from the ingestion of ayahuasca, the vine depicted in the left-hand corner of the painting,

this image relies on visual references from both Indigenous culture and Western science fiction. Visible in the centre, for example, is a shape that resembles a UFO. Peruvian shamanism has been influenced by both Catholic Christianity and contemporary culture.

PROFILE
PLANT TEACHERS

The scientific world sees plants as biological organisms belonging to the natural world, but from a shamanic point of view they can be considered teachers and, at the same time, helpers or assistants from the supernatural realms. Shamans talk about the knowledge accessed via ASCs achieved through the ingestion of parts of certain plants in terms of the relationship between master and pupil. Plants (the masters) facilitate shamans' (the pupils') work because they take shamans to unexpected areas of the universe that they would not be aware of if it wasn't for the help of these other-than-human beings. The knowledge these plants possess is what makes them essential allies in the practice of shamanism in many parts of the world.

TOBACCO
Tobacco is important among current Indigenous peoples of Brazil and in shamanic cultures worldwide. Tobacco is smoked, ingested, or brewed into a tea. Its powerful visions are sought by shamans to diagnose illnesses and to cure patients. Tobacco smoke brings prayers to the spirits.

MESCAL
Mescal beans from the Texas mountain laurel, which is native to northern Mexico and southern USA, have been used for their psychotropic properties since prehistory. Depictions of visions derived from the ingestion of the beans are among the world's most elaborate and vibrant expressions of shamans' ASCs.

COHOBA
Cohoba is the name the Arawakan inhabitants of the pre-Columbian Antilles gave to the pulverized seeds of the Anadenanthera tree. Bodily effects resulting from the ingestion of cohoba are vividly represented in Taíno art, for example the copious production of mucus and tears visible on the face of the figure on page 191.

SAN PEDRO CACTUS
Among the pre-Columbian peoples of the Andes, the San Pedro cactus was a sacred plant and had a central role in achieving ASCs. San Pedro, like some other cactaceae, contains the alkaloid mescaline, which can produce hallucinogenic effects. It was used in shamanic rituals and possibly by oracles performing in the temples of Chavín de Huántar in Peru.

AYAHUASCA
Popularized by a recent mounting interest in shamanism, ayahuasca has been used by tropical Indigenous South American peoples looking for shamanic insight for centuries. The tea, which is brewed with additional plants and roots, is today also consumed for therapeutic reasons, as it appears to benefit people suffering from depression or addiction.

PEYOTE
Peyote has been used to achieve ASCs among Indigenous peoples from the USA and Mexico since prehistory. The syncretic, Christian-based religion called Native American Church uses peyote as a replacement for sacred wafer, which is ingested in the ritual of communion. In the USA the use of peyote is allowed in the context of Indigenous religious practice.

DATURA
Shamans with datura pods in their hands appear in the rock art of northern Mexico and southern USA. Datura was also used by Indigenous Californians who administered it during shamanic initiation rituals. The visionary effects of this plant seem to have also been known among ancient Indo-Europeans.

AMANITA MUSCARIA
The use of the *Amanita muscaria* mushroom among Siberian shamans has been reported since the 18th century, but its use may pre-date this. Representations of mushrooms are not common in this region, but are frequent in the Americas, where they have been used among the Nahua and their predecessors.

HEMP
Excavations of a 2,500-year-old cemetery in China in 2019 confirmed Herodotus's claims in *Histories* that Scythian nomads used hemp and opium to achieve ASCs. This plant's seeds were sprinkled over hot stones to release the fumes responsible for a change in consciousness.

< Zār musicians, Cairo, Egypt, 2022
Rhythmic drumming and hypnotic beats help participants achieve a trance state to exorcize the demons that possess them. Zār trances help expel forces internal to the person in need of healing, whereas shamanic trances help shamans to leave their own bodies in search of cures and solutions.

> Trance during a Zār ceremony, Salakh, Iran, 2015
Zār possession is often used as an example in the argument for a distinction between spirit possession and shamanism. The healing effects of the drum temporarily alleviate the ailments of the subject tormented by malevolent spirits. Such dissociation may be analogous to working through traumas in psychoanalysis.

and dead ancestors, fetching human souls from the clutches of an evil entity, or visiting faraway places to spy on an enemy all require the staging of a seance. In the shamanic world, it is the most effective way to resolve a problem, or put an end to a conflict.

Several European eyewitnesses doubted the authenticity of shamanic seances, which they perceived as staged, contrived and artificial. Confessions of shamans feigning trances do exist, fuelling Western scepticism. Yet there may be an analogy here with the role of placebo in Western medicine: even shamans who only pretend to go into a trance may still provide the community with a solution to a problem, and recorded cases show that they can do so successfully.

Shamans judiciously choose their techniques according to the aim and purpose of their journey. Finding a lost object, and visiting the world of the dead, are different undertakings that demand varying levels and types of concentration. This is partially why scholarship is divided on the issue of definitions, because agreeing on the nature of these differences ultimately determines what counts as shamanism.

Classic theories of shamanism that follow the ideas of the historian of religions Mircea Eliade (1907–1986) promote the notion that shamans intentionally enter an ASC to communicate with beings that live in the metaphysical planes of the universe. Shamans' deliberate decision to stage a seance situates their

Jacques Torregano, woman dancing in a trance at a Santeria meeting, Cuba, 1992
Some Afro-American religions incorporate ASCs in their practice, usually in the form of spirit possession.

practice in contrast to those who haphazardly serve as hosts for spirits and those that experience amnesia as a result of possession.

Whether all these experiences fall under the umbrella of shamanism has not yet been resolved. Some scholars regard as shamanic any regions where ritual specialists fall into a different state of consciousness against their will, or claim to be possessed by spirits or other identities. Examples are societies of North and East Africa, where possession cults such as Zār bear some formal similarities with Siberian and American shamanism. For example, Zār followers go into a trance following sessions of rhythmic drumming, but they are believed to be possessed by spirits, and although the rituals are conducted in the context of healing a person (usually a woman) from tormenting spirits, it is the subject who goes into a trance and not the healer. The same happens in parts of southern Italy where women called *tarantate* ('women bitten by tarantulas'), fall to the ground after performing a frenzied dance to the sound of rhythmic drumming called *tarantella*.

PROFILE
SPECIALISTS
WHO USE ASCS

Though shamans make ASCs a defining trait of their social role, not all of the many ritual specialists who employ ASCs are shamans. The member of the Tambor de Mina religion pictured below, for example, is in a trance but cannot be called a shaman. In most societies, certain individuals conduct ceremonies to connect with invisible beings, but often during these

148   THE INTANGIBLE — 2 — *Communication Between Realities*

interactions subjects relinquish their control over the body to make room for spirits that possess or speak through them. Observers may converse with these incorporeal entities during the ritual, but, in some cases, the subject does not remember what they said. Shamans, by contrast, can report with clarity what they have seen or heard during their trances.

VIETNAMESE SPIRIT MEDIUM
Spirit mediumship is a form of ASC found in Vietnam and beyond. Mediums may receive messages through visions or auditory and tactile sensations. Through ASC, Vietnamese mediums speak with the dead and help lost spirits to reconnect with their families.

HAITIAN VODOU
People possessed during Afro-Haitian Vodou rituals are said to be straddled by spirits. They lose consciousness for variable periods of time. Their ASC differs from a shamanic ASC as the person becomes the vessel for the entity that is said to mount them, like a human mounts a horse.

NECHUNG ORACLE
Since the 11th century, Tibetan Buddhism has featured a diviner who prophesies for the Dalai Lama. The Nechung oracle is aided by assistants who relay what he whispers while in a state of trance. He has the power of clairvoyance, which is activated while he experiences an ASC.

BENANDANTI
In the 16th century, the *benandanti* of northern Italy fought battles against evil creatures in their dreams. They described their spirit journeys to the Catholic inquisitors who persecuted them as devil worshippers. When they can be controlled, lucid dreams are another form of ASC.

AMAZONIAN SHAMAN
ASC can be used by individuals to enable them to adopt the perspective of other species. Many Amazonian Indigenous groups use psychotropic agents to help them achieve this state. Whether a jaguar or a tapir, shamans assume an animal's perspective by temporarily turning into them.

SAN HEALER
San shamans of southern Africa enter ASCs to receive *n/om*, a numinous cosmic power that takes over during seances and is conceived as heat that enters the shaman's body and makes them shake and tremble. Shamans that experience *n/om* gain the ability to heal.

149   THE INTANGIBLE — 2 — *Communication Between Realities*

It is important when discussing shamanic seances today to take into consideration the contexts in which distinct episodes of trance, stupor or rapture happen. In contrast to *tarantate* or Zār followers, shamans are the ones who heal the patients after the trance is over; they are not the ones that undergo therapy in the form of possession.

Observing and determining what happens during any of these episodes may be difficult because an unbiased judgment can only be made based on what the subjects of these episodes disclose, and these accounts may be confusing and at times contradictory. Shamans who go into a trance to fight demons, spiritual enemies or evil entities do not always manage to retain their power, for example, and may at times succumb to the strength of their opponents. In such instances it may be appropriate to say that they are possessed. Yet, on anthropological and sociological grounds, these occasional occurrences should be considered of a different nature to 'possession'. Regardless of the extent to which shamans may temporarily lose grip on their power, they usually regain it and remember what happened while they were temporarily dissociated from ordinary reality.

More importantly, possessed individuals do not perform the same social role as shamans and do not hold the same central place in the community. Spirit mediums possessed by entities, though speaking with or through the dead much like shamans do, do not carry out healing, and neither do they perform most of the other roles that shamans have in a society. Spirit possession, oracular divination or temporary loss of consciousness may in most cases follow a rather rigid ritual structure, but they are episodic affairs that, while bearing resemblances to shamanic seances, may be considered different phenomena. Although, in the case of shamans, trances and possession may not be easily separated, it is ultimately what practitioners do for the community that establishes most clearly what counts as shamanism. The shamanic seance, so central to the life of the social group, is not just a fight over evil forces that threaten social balance and cosmic unity, or bring illnesses, but is also a moment when a society comes together, strengthening a sense of identity and solidarity.

> *pages 152–53*
> Anderson Debernardi,
> *Adan Visionario*, 2015
> Christian and shamanic references merge in this painting of Adam and a shaman. The image draws inspiration from visions experienced after the ingestion of ayahuasca, which may be used in shamanic therapies.

Franco Pinna, from *The Therapeutic Dance Cycle of Maria di Nardò* (detail), 1959

Musicians performing the rhythm of the tarantella are said to heal the tarantata ('the woman bitten by the tarantula'), who lies in a state of dissociation. Southern Italian tarantism may have its roots in ancient Greek cults, where women possessed by the god Dionysus danced in a raptured frenzy until exhausted or unconscious.

THE INTANGIBLE — 2 — *Communication Between Realities*

INCORPOREAL DIMENSIONS

'As soon as one of the supernatural powers or a shaman
came secretly to kill him, the shaman Mouth At Each End
sent his supernatural helpers...or if a supernatural power
came up flying through the air, Thunderbird and Lightning with
Hail would destroy him. Therefore the supernatural beings
from all parts of the world could not kill this shaman.'

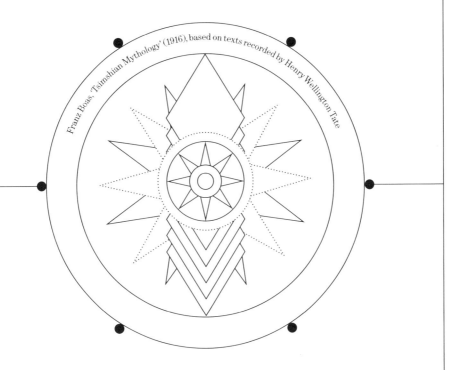

Franz Boas, 'Tsimshian Mythology' (1916), based on texts recorded by Henry Wellington Tate

Among the things that separate shamans from ordinary humans
is their ability to actively interact with invisible dimensions. Their realities
are based on an unequal distribution of power between a multiplicity
of beings, of which humans are one type. Most beings, including spirits,
the dead and other entities, display volition and can take from
or bestow power to humans according to the laws of reciprocity
that structure shamanic worldviews.

Perceiving the existence of invisible dimensions beyond phenomenal reality is a trait shared by all human societies since prehistory. Empirical evidence, embodied experiences and observation indicate that we are not just flesh and blood; we breathe, imagine and feel. We have memories, dreams and thoughts. Existential questions related to the place of humans in this world are partially shaped by reflections upon life's intangible aspects, and solutions to explain their existence vary greatly. For example, while in the Christian tradition the body is the vehicle for the soul, shamanic societies may be more flexible as to the number of souls that inhabit one person and conceive of the body as having a permeable surface. In some cultures, the existence of more than one soul explains the existence of shadows, or how persons can travel to incorporeal dimensions when asleep and still remain alive in both immaterial and material realms at once.

Animistic frameworks at the base of shamanic beliefs and practices provide the background that enables us to understand how shamans interpret and explain the world. Such frameworks include the existence of incorporeal entities and dimensions, and shamans must become familiar with these in order to resolve concrete problems, from illness to lack of food. The difficulties and obstacles of ordinary life cannot be resolved with purely material solutions, according to these ways of thinking, because their origins are usually of a different nature. Modern shamans, for example, may be perfectly well aware of the physical causes of disease (bacterial, viral or neurological), but for them everything that affects humans is traceable to a spiritual source.

In a shamanic framework, disruptions of the natural order are caused by malevolent forces that act beyond the visible. The cosmos is affected by the existence of intangible beings and energies that act upon human life, and we can recognize this in the strong emphasis on everything that is incorporeal and invisible in all shamanic cultural expressions. Shamans operate in a reality populated by spirits, disembodied other-than-human entities, demons and dead people. At different times these may be witches, wandering ghosts,

⟨ *page 154*
Mapuche *machi*,
Araucania, Chile,
19th century
The machi *stands on a wooden ladder (*rewe*) that connects her to the upper realms and their inhabitants. Detachment from the earth facilitates this shaman's communication with intangible entities.*

László Forbáth, shaman fighting invisible forces, Mongolia, 1934

Shamans muster techniques that enable them to tune into dimensions not accessible to ordinary humans. Even in these circumstances shamans are usually able to retain some memory of the events, which they either retell or turn into visual records.

157 THE INTANGIBLE — 3 — *Incorporeal Dimensions*

< Jesse Oonark, *A Shaman's Helping Spirits*, 1971
This Inuit shaman is surrounded by animal helpers. They may appear in visions or real-life encounters. They announce their presence to the shaman to confirm their commitment to the covenant that mutually binds them.

> Tlingit Atlatl (spear-thrower), Pacific Northwest Coast of North America, 1750–1800
This ancient weapon fell into disuse after the introduction of bows and arrows, yet retained its power as a spiritual weapon. Probably never used in battle, this example may have served the ceremonial purpose of throwing magical darts at the shaman's enemies.

displeased ancestors or enemy shamans competing for power and dominance. Whether generated by rivalry, envy or self-preservation, the effects of evil forces, curses and spells are felt in the community and shamans will be asked to intervene to restore balance. Powerful accounts and even rare photographs of shamans' spiritual fights give us a vibrant picture of the reality of these battles against malicious entities.

The strenuous efforts made by shamans during these conflicts are evident in the energetic performances staged during public seances. With the help of their spiritual aides, shamans will cast unwanted entities back to their own realms. Alternatively, they may try to appease these beings with flattering words, or in the worst cases, directly engage in dangerous fights with them. In places such as the Amazon and Siberia, shamans may throw invisible darts at their enemies in a display of strength and unparalleled vehemence. In the Northwest Coast of North America, specific implements are known to have been made for this purpose: atlatls (spear-throwers) that send magic projectiles against the shaman's enemies. Shamans may also fight their opponents in spirit wrestling, or struggle to disentangle themselves from dangerous

Embera shaman, Panama, 2012
Botanical knowledge is essential for shamanic therapeutics. The active properties of plants are intrinsically linked to their role as helpers with their own wisdom and agency.

magical traps. These performative expressions reveal the central place held by immaterial entities in the physical world and demonstrate to human onlookers how shamans deal with metaphysical dimensions.

While most entities have names and may be summoned when these are spoken aloud, not all are personified; they are simply known to exist. Oral traditions reference them in songs, invocations, prayers and evocations. During seances, they are addressed in conversations, altercations and verbal clashes that happen in dimensions visible only to the shaman.

On returning from their spiritual journeys, shamans may describe the otherworldly landscapes they have seen. It has been suggested that what once were considered imaginary travels may correspond to what is known as 'remote viewing'. Though not universally accepted as a proven scientific fact, this phenomenon has attracted the interest of many scientists and some have devised experiments to try to demonstrate the reality of such a paranormal ability. Regardless, for shamans this is a real skill that enables them to travel across real spaces, as well as to cosmic regions above and below the human, material dimension.

Hornbill (*kenyalang*) sculpture, Sarawak, Malaysia
Central to important ceremonies, hornbill figures such as this one represent intermediaries between the world of the living and the incorporeal dimensions of deities and spirits.

In these out-of-body travels, shamans are frequently accompanied by invisible helpers who keep them safe during the seance and assist them to make a smooth return to ordinary reality. There, human assistants attend to their needs, for example interpreting their accounts, handing them ritual implements, singing or playing musical instruments.

It is important to recognize the distinction between spirit guides and spirit helpers in order to understand the interactions between humans and other-than-human beings in shamanism. Spirit guides may be encountered in dreams, and shamans meet them only in incorporeal form when the shaman achieves a disembodied dimension. Guides are personal to individual shamans and will accompany them for life.

Helpers, instead, are occasional aides that are called upon when particular circumstances dictate. They may be human or other-than-human. Not infrequently, they may be embodied in animals who act as messengers that can mediate on behalf of the shaman or deliver messages to incorporeal realms. A case in point are birds in Siberia, North America and South East Asia, where avian iconography is common in shamanic contexts.

Simon Tookoome, *I am Always Thinking About the Animals*, 1974
Inuit shamans rely on the help of different animals and other-than-human entities to carry out their work. This shaman figure features multiple faces, as is common in Inuit masks, surrounded by reindeer, bears, wolves and geese.

Plants may also be helpers (see pages 144–45), but tend not to belong to just one practitioner. They can be consulted by any shaman for a diagnosis, or to answer a question. There are also invisible helpers that do not manifest themselves, but are known to shamans. Their incorporeality does not make them any less real; in fact, their help may be essential to a shaman's success. Both guides and helpers may have a visible form, such as an animal or plant, but it is their spiritual power that protects shamans in their perilous activities.

Spirit helpers become a shaman's main protector by virtue of the pledge made between them. This usually happens at the time of initiation, or during traumatic ordeals that will determine a person's life as a shaman. Indeed, becoming a shaman is not a choice, but rather a calling, one that is determined by forces beyond a person's control. Visions, dreams and mystical encounters, made during prolonged illnesses or near-death experiences, will show the soon-to-be shaman who will be his or her guide. These episodes are the precondition to becoming a shaman in most parts of

DECODING INUIT MASKS

In North America's precolonial Arctic regions, masks were variably used in shamanic contexts such as rituals, dances and burials. These instruments, in all their variety, form an extremely rich archive of imagery that reflects shamanic views of the inhabitants of the universe and its composition. From purely abstract to extravagantly surreal, they often depict hybrid beings and shamans' helpers. Christianity prohibited the ritual use of masks, and so today most of the old specimens are stored in museums and private collections.

HANDS
Hands often decorate Yup'ik masks. Some, such as this one, are thumbless. Others also have a hole in the palm to convey that spirit helpers are unable to hold onto animal spirits and so are willing to let the animals flow abundantly into the living world.

HOLES
Some masks, such as this Yup'ik one, include holes that shamans travel through to retrieve lost souls, fight evil spirits or talk to the spirits of animals. Masks are more than symbolic, they are concrete aids that help shamans in their journeys.

HOOPS
Yup'ik masks from Alaska frequently feature hoops that encircle the central figure. They can vary in number and are called *ellanguaq*. They represent the part of the universe where animal spirits live or, alternatively, the sky's layers.

MAGGOTS
This mask from the Ipiutak culture of Point Hope, Alaska (100 BCE– 800 CE), can be recomposed, signifying shape-shifting. At the sides of the mouth are two maggots, which are common shamans' helpers as they can transform and withstand the cold.

DUALISM
Alaskan animal masks may feature human faces on their bodies, as in this late 19th-century mask, or emerging from a beak or muzzle. This device reveals the personhood of the animal or its ability to shape-shift into a human (and vice versa).

DISTORTED FACE
Spirits may appear with faces that are asymmetrical. Such characters are common in Inuit oral traditions, and this is how they are depicted on Yup'ik shamanic masks. They represent the ambivalent essence of reality and the duplicitous nature of all beings.

163   THE INTANGIBLE — 3 — *Incorporeal Dimensions*

the known shamanic world. Once shamans receive their spirit guides, they will be able to use the powers they are endowed with to their advantage and, in turn, must respect special taboos, dietary prescriptions or certain behaviours to honour the covenant.

Gods, nature spirits, spirit helpers, guides, ancestors and demons are frequently depicted in art. To external viewers, some of these representations may appear as surreal, imaginary, abstract or fantastic, but in a shamanic mindset these are manifestations of very real beings. Though depicted for the benefit of humans in the dimension of the five senses, many of these other-than-human persons literally enter the effigies created for them so that they can show themselves to the naked eye.

Spirit guardians, for example, are known to protect shamans' graves in several shamanic societies. Their fierce looks may not resemble anything that most humans have ever seen in real life, but their unusual features are taken to be a faithful reproduction of their appearance. Aggressive horned figures mounted on wooden pedestals from the Eastern Zhou period in China (770–221 BCE) are one such example. Mixing anatomical details from felines, stags and humans, and showing distinctive features such as bulging eyes and protruding tongues, several of these statues recovered from funerary contexts have been interpreted as being 'supernatural' beings whose role was to guard the tombs where they were placed. In a similar fashion, figures with human-like faces and terrifying fangs stand in front of tombs of the San Agustín culture from Colombia (1–900 CE) as a perennial warning to trespassers.

Masks and other implements, too, may display depictions of a shaman's guides. Among the Siberian Evenk, anthropomorphic silhouettes of the shaman's aides are stitched onto aprons worn during seances. In the Pacific Northwest, they are depicted on shamanic masks used in curing rituals. Among Mongolian-speaking peoples, effigies of protectors are shown wearing crowns of spirits encircling their heads. A similar concept can be found in some statuettes produced in Brazil by the Santarem culture, in which sitting figures are depicted wearing a headband made

Shaman's grave, Chilkat, Alaska, c. 1895

Carved figures guard the burial site of this Tlingit shaman. Tomb guardians are a type of shamanic helper. Although these guardians are supposed to keep human intruders at bay, they also act in invisible dimensions to protect the shaman's incorporeal elements.

165   THE INTANGIBLE —3— *Incorporeal Dimensions*

DECODING THE SITTING SHAMAN

Stools have been used in the shamanic practices of South and Central America and the Caribbean since pre-Columbian times. This instrument helps the shaman align themselves to the cosmic axis that connects the universe's multiple layers, metaphorically turning shamans into embodiments of this concept. Variably decorated with cosmological or mythical symbols and designs, stools are often represented in art and continue to be used in regions where shamanism is still widely practised. This 1300–1500 CE Tairona ocarina from Colombia shows a shaman sitting on his stool. He displays a crocodile's muzzle, or possibly a bat's, which is an indication that he is shape-shifting.

166   THE INTANGIBLE — 3 — *Incorporeal Dimensions*

TAÍNO EFFIGY
Pre-Columbian Taíno artists of the Antilles occasionally represented a common scene: a shaman sitting on their stool after ingesting cohoba, the pulverized seeds of the Anadenanthera tree, a potent stimulant that would have aided shamans in their spiritual journeys.

QUIMBAYA LIME FLASK
This Early Quimbaya gold-alloy container from Colombia was used to store lime, an agent that reacts with coca leaves to release psychotropic chemicals. It portrays a female shaman sitting on a stool with her eyes closed, holding two vines of a plant.

SANTAREM FIGURINE
Produced in Brazil between 1000 and 1700 CE, this figure shows all the features of a shaman. His elbows are resting on his knees, his eyes are closed in meditation or trance, and he is wearing a crown of stringed *muiraquitãs*, precious stone amulets representing frogs or other animals.

NARIÑO STATUETTE
Andean peoples have been using coca leaves for centuries. One way in which they are used is to divine the future. This pre-Columbian statue from Colombia depicts a sitting shaman who is clearly chewing coca, as is apparent from the visible lump in his cheek.

CHINESCO FIGURE
This Mexican Nayarit figurine in the Chinesco style (100–400 CE) shows the classic pose of the sitting shaman. His body painting and attire suggest he had a high rank. Shamans were often community leaders in many parts of the pre-Columbian Americas.

SHAFT TOMB FIGURINE
The pose of this 200 BCE–500 CE Nayarit figure is a common position held by shamans in trance states. Western Mexican pre-Columbian cultures may have used peyote to help their shamans reach an ASC. Peyote continues to be used in the same region by the Huichol people.

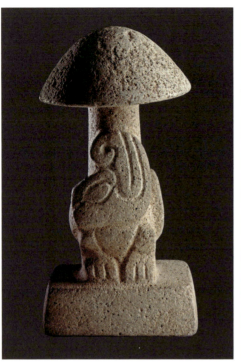 

< **Maya statue of a mushroom, Kaminaljuyu, Guatemala, 2000 BCE–250 CE**
Mushrooms may have been used for their psychoactive properties in Central America since the period when this statue was made. More recently, their use was recorded among the Mazatec people of Mexico, indicating a possible continuity with the ancient practice.

> **Anthropomorphic statues, Ometepe Island, Nicaragua, 1100–1300 CE**
Depictions of animals towering over humans are found throughout the tropical Americas. Zoomorphic headdresses are the manifestations of animal doubles, spiritual helpers or protective guides.

of stringed frog amulets, possibly referencing some species whose subcutaneous glands excrete a highly potent chemical used in shamanic rituals. Historically, Indigenous American peoples from the Arctic to Argentina have produced many representations of shamanic helpers. Particularly impressive are pectorals representing shamans flanked by their assistants, created by Chibcha-speaking peoples from Colombia and Panama using gold–copper alloys called *tumbaga*.

Animals are usually depicted more frequently than plants or invisible spirits. Yet representations of vines, trees, branches, roots, foliage and mushrooms also appear in shamanic visual expressions. It is not always possible to distinguish representations of the physical reality from depictions of the essence of things. For example, a shamanic coat from the Amur River in Siberia features the image of the three cosmic trees of the Nanai (or Goldi), the people from which it was acquired in 1900. The image is based on natural trees. Phenomenal reality may help us to find visual

Golden pendant depicting vines and plants, Panama, 400–700 CE
These spiral forms are common in the international style that connected Panama to Colombia. They frequently appear in the hands of performing shamans or as decorations on their headdresses.

Early Quimbaya lime flask, Colombia, 500 BCE–700 CE
Containers in the shape of gourds were used to store lime, an activating agent that enhances coca's effects on the body.

metaphors for ideas or abstract concepts, so in some designs it is possible to recognize familiar objects. For example, soul flight can be visualized through wings or feathers. From a shamanic perspective, the significance of the designs is in their representation of the abstract concept and not in their faithful depiction of the world.

Geometric and abstract themes found widely in art produced in shamanic contexts, too, are depictions of incorporeal dimensions. It can be hard for modern viewers to interpret what exactly they may represent. Attempts at explaining these motifs scientifically were advanced by David Lewis-Williams (1934–) and Thomas A. Dowson (1964–) in their proposal of a neuro psychological model for identifying entoptic phenomena in rock art. Meaning 'inside the eye', the term entoptic has been employed to describe the phenomenon by which the retina produces geometric forms during the first stages of an ASC. Though the entoptic theory has not been universally accepted, for many people in the West, the legitimacy of this physio-cognitive model roots ASCs in science, rendering shamanism more acceptable to those who need to grasp this socio-religious phenomenon from a rational point of view.

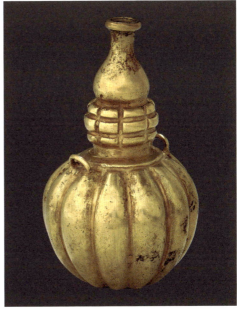

PROFILE
ENTOPTIC PHENOMENA AND SHAMANISM

The theory of entoptic phenomena is based on human neurophysiology and offers a scientific framework that may explain the reoccurrence of certain designs and motifs in rock art. Entoptic means 'inside the eye' and can refer to the shapes seen in the early stages of an ASC. These may be grids, lines, nested chevrons, spirals, meshes, waves or bursts of light. Archaeologists David Lewis-Williams and Thomas A. Dowson, who created the table opposite, argue that many symbols found in rock art, despite varying in exact form, have their origins in the human physio-cognitive function.

The table reproduces six categories of entoptic phenomena in columns A and B and compares these to motifs that occur in southern African San rock art engravings (column C) and paintings (column D), and Coso rock art from Native California (column E). Examples of some of the designs are reproduced below.

Not everyone is convinced that these abstract forms rendered in rock art always have a shamanic character. Ideas and experiences may be visually communicated through symbols and geometric figures without having an origin in ASC.

GRIDS (I)
These c. 8000 BCE grids, carved at Mont-Rouget, France, invite us to question the context in which they were made. Shamans are often considered the first artists, but proving their existence based on these carvings is difficult.

CHEVRONS (IE)
The cross-hatching and chevrons carved, c. 75,000 years ago, into this red ochre from Blombos Cave in South Africa may not be linked to shamanism, but shamanism has been positively identified among the southern African San peoples.

PARALLEL LINES (II)
The Altai Kalbak-Tash petroglyphs were made between 3000 and 1000 BCE. We no longer know the visual principles used here, so they are hard to decipher. Perhaps they depicted something from the real world that is obscure to observers.

170 THE INTANGIBLE — 3 — *Incorporeal Dimensions*

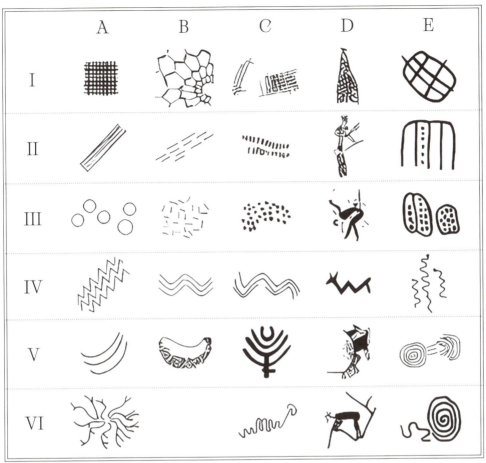

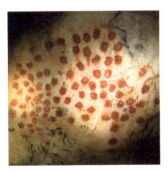

DOTS (III)
Staring at the sun, watching a waterfall, focusing on ripples in water and other experiences may cause entoptic phenomena that resemble the dots in the Chauvet Cave in France, dating from 37,000 to 33,000 BCE.

ZIGZAGS (IV)
Entoptic phenomena may not be the basis for rock art, despite similarities between them and designs produced by shamanic cultures. In this prehistoric Colombian painting, zigzags may represent the cosmic anaconda.

CIRCLES (VI)
Circles, such as these ones from California, are very common in rock art. The simplicity of this form allowed different cultures to convey a variety of meanings. In this case, they may be linked to shamanism practised in the region.

171   THE INTANGIBLE — 3 — *Incorporeal Dimensions*

PROFILE
AMULETS AND CHARMS

Protective charms, amulets and miniature objects are carried by shamans in everyday life and during seances. Some of these are reproductions of things that people commonly use, such as knives, mirrors or hammers. Others may be natural items imbued with supernatural power, including dried roots, parts of animals, feathers, bones or small pebbles, or items specifically made for a special purpose. The antler below has been carved into the form of an unidentified creature, and would have been used as a shaman's amulet. It was made between 1775 and 1865 in Sitka, Alaska.

INUIT PROTECTIVE BELT
Small weapons are sometimes strapped to the belts of Inuit shamans to help them fight invisible enemies met during a soul flight. Siberian shamans may use different instruments as weapons, which they usually strap or sew onto their robes.

CHUKCHI EFFIGY
Siberian wooden effigies, such as this one, may be used during reindeer-hunting rituals, as home protectors or for divination. They usually represent males, but groups of figures can include a female, representing the mythical woman of the sky.

ALASKAN INUIT AMULET
A variety of figurines were part of the toolkit of Inuit shamans who used them in different rituals. Amulets may be carried on the person, attached to implements or even fastened to visors, as the Aleut did. This example, carved from ivory, appears to depict a seal.

CHINESE BI
Though the actual role of jade *bi*, such as this *c.* 100 BCE example, is not known, their resemblance to the hoops used by Siberian shamans suggests that they may have had cosmological meanings; perhaps they were a point of access to supernatural realms.

KULAI AMULET
It is impossible to tell exactly what amulets from the Kulai culture of the Ob River basin, Siberia, were used for. Some of them bear resemblance to later items from neighbouring regions. This bronze anthropomorphic figure dates from 300 BCE–200 CE.

EVENK EFFIGY
A rich inventory of cut-out figures, such as this anthropomorphic example, and abstract shapes help Evenk shamans while they are in a trance. Birds, which feature prominently in Siberian lore as both messengers and mounts, are often depicted.

173   THE INTANGIBLE — 3 — *Incorporeal Dimensions*

Shamans and Neo-Shamans, by contrast, disagree with purely scientific readings of shamanic practices and beliefs. Recent accounts collected among contemporary practitioners confirm their conviction of the reality of visions, in blatant disregard of what science can prove. They argue that the existence of certain dimensions of reality cannot be demonstrated scientifically, but can only be experienced. Such statements are received in some quarters with a degree of scepticism, especially when they come from practitioners who have only recently adopted the practice of Neo-Shamanism, shedding their previous convictions to enter the world of animistic thinking. Doubts about the authenticity of these beliefs may be contrasted with how the existence of spirits and otherworldly entities is talked about and perceived in places where shamanism was practised before colonialism. In Scandinavian countries, for example, neo-traditional forms of shamanism emerged on the basis of old practices as a decolonizing response to the encroaching forces of modernization and secularization. There, evidence of cultural continuity, and the recovery of practices once banned under oppressive regimes, seem better to support the belief in incorporeal dimensions so central to shamans and their contemporary followers.

The degree to which these contrasting views can be reconciled is a matter of ongoing debate. New forms of shamanism will continue to assert the validity of their beliefs, whether adhering to old formulas, or integrating new sources of inspiration and practice. Syncretic spiritualities have historically sprung out of encounters between incompatible religious principles and theologies the world over. Like the various forms of Neo-Shamanism recorded today, beliefs and practices that emerged out of these interactions were opportunistically reworked in creative combinations. For example, beings and entities experienced in incorporeal dimensions were translated for local publics through foreign ideas and principles. In Neo-Shamanism and Core Shamanism, exotic ideas were merged in new formations that became convincing antidotes to modernity's materialism and disenchantment.

Nanai shaman's ritual clothing, Amur River region, Russia/China border

The tree that decorates this garment grows at the centre of the Earth and is climbed by the shaman to reach the sky. The drawing is the physical manifestation of this invisible plant. Iconographies such as this encapsulate the shamanic world and its cosmology.

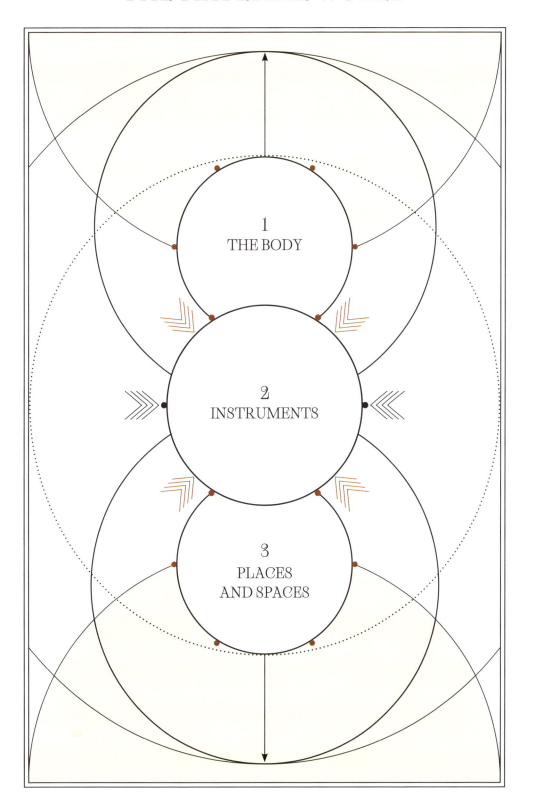

THE BODY

'[This] branch of shamanism…is called "soft man being" (yırka´-la´ul-va´ırgın); "soft man" (yırka´-la´ul) meaning a man transformed into a being of a softer sex.'

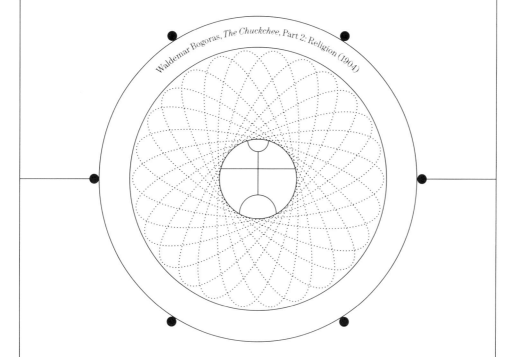

Waldemar Bogoras, *The Chuckchee, Part 2: Religion* (1904)

Shamans inhabit bodies that are different from those of other humans. Their ability to cross boundaries means that they can choose to turn into different beings. In so doing, they transcend the rules of physics and the categories assigned to humans according to ethnicity, gender and even species. Shamans' extraordinary powers set them apart from everyone else. They are treated with awe and ambivalence due to the in-betweenness that makes them special.

In many traditional cultures, occupations and tasks are usually assigned according to gender. Social responsibilities and prerogatives are allocated to males, females or intersex people according to the characteristics that a given society ascribes to particular bodies. The identifying features are usually the genitals, or secondary sexual characteristics, but in a minority of cases a society may rely on marks on the body, or special behaviours, to assign specific roles to individuals – notably shamans.

By and large, shamans are classified as a separate category of people: those who display unique behaviours and predispositions that everyone recognizes as out of the ordinary. Typical characteristics may belong to a particular gender. Some of the shamans' peculiarities may be detected at birth, but a potential shaman may also be recognized later in life if, for example, the person's demeanour, speech or mannerisms change following a sudden illness, a traumatic event or a near-death experience. These are usually the preconditions of becoming a shaman: the person's life temporarily transitions into the invisible dimension of death as a result of physical disease, experiencing trauma, or episodic mental or psychological conditions. Accounts of prolonged sicknesses affecting people who later become shamans are common. Some individuals experience dissociative states for months or years, after which they can no longer refuse the calling, lest they die. These in-between states signal a rupture with normal life and indicate to the ailing person that a new phase of their existence is about to start.

Soon-to-be shamans may see themselves undergoing unspeakable torments in vivid dreams, visions and other states caused by illness. During these critical periods, experiences of dismemberment are typical. Terrifying personal narratives report people being disarticulated, defleshed and sometimes even eaten by otherworldly beings. Suffering, in those cases, becomes the indelible mark of shamanhood. Eventually, the body is recomposed and the shaman emerges, made new, from the ordeal. Dismemberment can be seen as a metaphor for death and rebirth,

‹ *page 176*
Edward Curtis, man wearing a maskette, Nunivak Island, Alaska, 1929
Masks belong to a shamanic worldview in which animals, humans, plants and atmospheric phenomena actively interact as sentient beings. Material culture is an instrument of communication between species.

‹ *page 178*
Marie Antoinette Czaplicka, Tungus shaman in ceremonial dress, c. 1920
The unusual position of the apron below the shaman's waist indicates that the photographer may have adjusted it to capture its details.

Nat, **Myanmar, 2003** — *The nats of Myanmar have been called shamans, although they connect with spirits through possession, not soul flight. While nats are mostly female, the in-betweenness of these figures and their role is frequently manifested in transgender and non-binary individuals.*

DECODING CASAS GRANDES SHAMAN

Common in the figurative expressions of the Mogollon culture of Mexico are effigies of smoking shamans, dating from 1150 to 1450 CE. Seated in a highly conventional pose, their markings are richly symbolic, relating to deities, maize and fertility. This *c*. 1200 CE jar was discovered at Casas Grandes, Chihuahua, and shows the use of tobacco, which helped shamans achieve Alternative States of Consciousness and fly to the furthest parts of the universe. There is no agreement on how these clay figurines might have been used.

1.

2.

3.

CYLINDER PIPE
Mogollon shamans used tobacco in their rituals. Several species grow in the Americas, but the most commonly used in traditional shamanic practice is *Nicotiana rustica*, due to its potency. Caribbean and Amazonian shamans, too, are known for their use of tobacco.

FACIAL MARKINGS
The V signs that decorate the shaman's face display a symbol commonly associated with corn kernels: a dot in a square. These visual references to maize can be found on objects from neighbouring regions where the people, like the Mogollon, were agriculturists.

CIRCLES WITH DOTS
The circles with dots at their centres painted on the shaman's legs and back are conventional signs for snake skin. When paired with feather symbols, they stand for the plumed serpent, an important being of Casas Grandes cosmology and mythology.

4.

5.

6.

SASH
This item of clothing, worn across the chest from shoulder to hip, is overwhelmingly associated with male figures in Casas Grandes iconography. Understood to be a symbol of status, its usage here may indicate the high position held by shamans in this society.

ZIGZAGS
This common motif appears in different guises in Casas Grandes shamanic iconography. It also recurs in other visual traditions. Usually associated with ASCs, in this region zigzags may equally signify snakes or lightning, common metaphors for rain and moisture.

KNEELING POSE
Interpreted as a part of divinatory rituals, the kneeling pose of this Casas Grandes figurine regularly reappears in the iconography of shamans of this region. Important knowledge from the intangible world was shared by shamans while they were in this position.

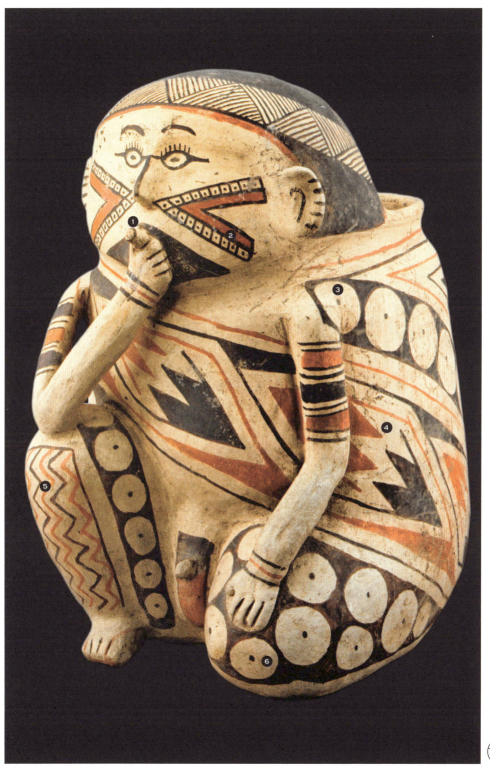

183   THE MATERIAL WORLD —1— *The Body*

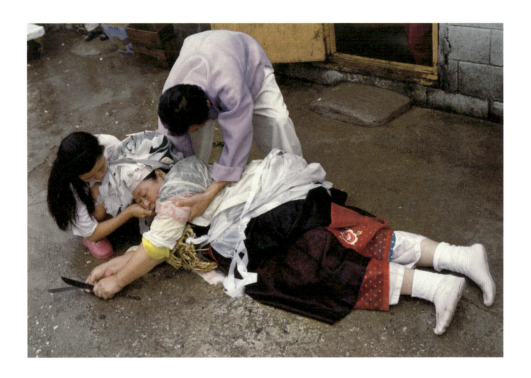

Mark de Fraeye, shamanic ritual, South Korea, 1995
A mudang *collapses during a trance and is aided by her helpers. Shamans' strenuous efforts often result in moments of dissociation, but they generally retain memories of their incorporeal voyages.*

a transitional stage in which the old personality is replaced by one endowed with new abilities and the potential to enhance innate skills.

As noted previously, early scholars concluded that shamans were mentally anomalous individuals, but this was based on reports of their behaviour under an ASC. During seances shamans might experience mood swings, roll on the floor, speak in tongues or act dramatically, all traits that led scholars and observers to diagnose shamans' mental states using the language of schizophrenia, hysteria or epilepsy. Around the end of the nineteenth century and in the early twentieth, anthropology's aspirations to become an exact science relied heavily on medicine and the emerging discipline of psychoanalysis. Both greatly influenced interpretations of the ethnographic material related to shamanism. However, none of the evidence reviewed in the last fifty years supports these once-popular perceptions.

Shamans' unique personae may be moulded not only by their behaviour or mental states but also by

184   THE MATERIAL WORLD —1— *The Body*

Buryat shaman's hands, Olkhon Island, Lake Baikal, Russia, 2000
Certain bodily features may indicate a child's special nature. They signal inherent shamanic abilities bestowed on them by agents of the spirit world.

distinctive physical features, such as having extra bones in their bodies, or being born en caul (with the amniotic sac unruptured). In their own societies, rather than being stigmatized or pathologized for being different, they are often accorded awe and respect – along with a degree of ambivalence. After all, shamans indisputably cross a multiplicity of social boundaries that are observed by most people.

Typically characterized by their ability to travel to invisible dimensions, shamans are not limited by the materiality of the body. They are simultaneously present in the flesh and yet able to take part in actions beyond the physical. Straddling reality's many layers, they embody paradox. Many of them transcend gender limitations. Not coincidentally, in some parts of the world shamans are considered a separate gender, as they manifest at once the bodies and behavioural characteristics of both normative genders. This feature can be perceived as transcending gender altogether, a concept well expressed in the many manifestations of shamanism associated with what in today's terms

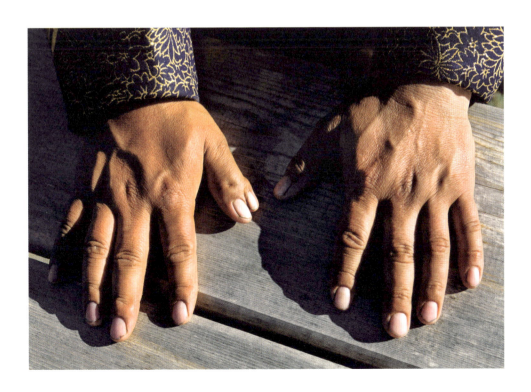

A Filipino *babaylan* named Papa Isio, 1907

Like in other Austronesian societies, babaylans crossed gender boundaries by wearing both female and male attire. They were spirit mediums and healers. Babaylan was originally an inherited profession, but a child could be selected to become one if they experienced severe diseases or trauma.

are called non-binary configurations of gender, sex and sexuality. Shamans may achieve this by adopting behaviours, speech, mannerisms and clothing from both the male and female repertoires normative in their own cultures. Nineteenth-century Indigenous California shamans would wear male attire, yet sport female jewelry and the typical woven hats of post-pubescent women. More recently, among the Zulu of South Africa, male neophytes aspiring to become *sangoma* (possessed healers) adopted female garb.

There are also reports from the Islamic world that confirm the practice of gender-crossing dress up to the mid-twentieth century. A famous case is that of the Uzbek shaman Tasmat Kholmatov, born in 1886), who after a sickness at the age of seven was compelled by the spirits to wear women's clothing for the rest of his life. He donned women's dresses, alongside male trousers, a man's skull cap and a beard. More instances of shamanic mixed attire have been reported throughout Asia, ranging from the Khorezm in Turkmenistan to the Kamchadal, the Koryak and the Chukchi of Siberia.

Examples from Asia, the Americas and even Europe indicate that, while transcending gender was not a prerequisite to becoming a shaman in these regions, belonging to both genders (or neither) is the embodiment of the condition of existing and operating in multiple dimensions. This typology of shamans has been recorded in many societies, yet how they might have been classified in their own languages is not always known. As a result, in some cases we only have translated descriptions for shamans, such as 'soft men' among the Chukchi of Siberia, or interpretations attributed by external observers to what they saw, as in the case of the 'transvestite doctors' in the Tolowa tribe of California. By contrast, local names for this class of spiritual practitioners have been recorded from, for example, the Philippines (*babaylan*) and Myanmar (*nat kadaw*), and among the Iban in Malaysia (*manang bali*), the Bugis of Indonesia (*bissu*), and the Mapuche of Chile (*machi*).

Most shamans retain their gender permanently, and their identities manifest themselves either from birth,

< **Seated figure, Greater Nicoya, Nicaragua, 800–1350 CE**
The abundance of figurines displaying characteristics of both sexes indicates the relevance of androgyny in this Central American culture. The figure may be a transforming shaman or a metaphor for transcending the boundaries typical of shamanic traditions across the Americas.

> **Androgynous figure, Punuk culture, Alaska, 800–1200 CE**
The notion that humans can change gender over a lifetime and that shamans inhabit a 'third gender' appears to be an old one, as is indicated by this effigy. Some Inuit myths report that androgynous shamans created all women.

as the result of spirits' guidance, or at the onset of puberty. However, changes of gender may occur during a lifetime and may be temporary. There are instances when transvestism is required in order to intercede with other-than-humans during seances. Chocó male shamans from Argentina, called *jaibaná*, must adopt feminine symbols to seduce the spirits they need to overpower. They are able to conquer their incorporeal enemies by (momentarily) becoming the object of the spirits' desire, while retaining their masculine personae. The unification of two genders into one gives the *jaibaná* power over other-than-human persons. Cases of gender transcendence or transformation are at one end of a wide spectrum of variations. At the other end of the continuum, by contrast, there are shamans who show essentializing bodily features. In some societies, like that of ancient China, a shaman's sex determined his or her abilities, which were believed to be inherent to being a male or a female. Texts such as the *Shuowen Jiezi* (a Chinese dictionary compiled

Rock art, Lascaux, France, 22,000–17,000 BCE
This image of a man facing a bison may exhibit shamans' excessive sexual energy and appetite. The figure has also been called a shaman because of his bird-like features, although this interpretation is controversial.

in the first century BCE) clearly state that women are innately predisposed to deal with formless entities and are more readily inclined to become possessed by spirits, whereas men are better at divination.

This essentialism is also visible in the many vivid demonstrations of masculinity expressed through art. Sexual potency is mostly attributed to male shamans. Representations of shamans flaunting erections, for example, have been recovered among the Taíno inhabitants of the pre-Columbian Antilles. In addition to symbolizing fertility, masculine arousal, partially the result of the ingestion of psychotropic plants, is linked to shamans' allegedly exceptional sexual appetite.

Shamans' sexuality has intrigued hosts of scholars, probably because of the conflation between transgendering practices and male homosexuality that was common in the home countries of European observers. These commentators projected familiar templates onto the social realities they encountered, thereby skewing our understanding of not only gender systems

DECODING TAÍNO SHAMAN FIGURE

Votive effigies called *zemis* were common among the pre-Columbian Taíno inhabitants of the Antilles. This *c.* 1256–1300 example is carved from guayacan and stands at 1.04 metres (3 feet 5 inches) tall. Though usually carved from wood, *zemis* may be made of different materials. Some of them were made from

1.

2.

3.

TEARS
Tears stream from the figure's eyes, signifying the effects of cohoba, a psychotropic substance used by Taíno shamans. The deep grooves of the tears suggest they may have been inlaid with precious materials. Some Taíno objects display gold foil in the eye sockets, for example.

MOUTH
Almost all Taíno shamanic sculptures represent figures showing their teeth. The repetition of this peculiar trait, as well as the deep eye sockets, may indicate that these are representations of skeletonized corpses, indicating a shaman's connection to their ancestors.

PROMINENT GENITALS
The prominence of the shaman's genitals indicates his sexual potency. This detail is also diagnostic of the ingestion of psychotropics, several of which cause erections and discharges from various orifices of the body.

4.

5.

6.

CALVES
These enlarged calves show the result of a common practice of tying intentionally tight ligatures below the knee. In several tropical societies of South America, this is a feminine trait that signifies fertility. Interestingly, here the male shaman conveys this meaning.

VERTEBRAL COLUMN
Taíno shaman sculptures emphasize the spine. The spine is a metaphor for the cosmic axis that connects the three levels of the Taíno universe: above, centre and below. Shamans embody this idea when sitting on their ritual stools, called *duho*, which align them to this axis.

STANCE
Taíno artists followed the natural shape of wood when carving figures. Here, the V shape of the branch lends a suitably belligerent stance to the shaman. Other such *zemis* are known, indicating that this was among the preferred modes of depicting shamans.

netted fibres and beads, and incorporated human skulls. Some of these statues were kept in ceremonial, communal houses, and some were kept as protectors inside the home. The few effigies that escaped the Spanish priests' bonfires display common traits that point to the shamanic nature of the imagery.

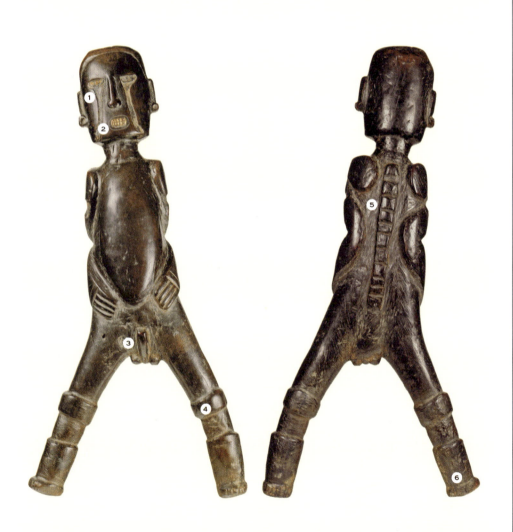

A. Abbas, a *mudang* (female shaman) cleanses a patient during a ritual, Seoul, Korea, 2007

Blades are used by Korean shamans to prove their mastery over matter. Shamans around the world perform feats of power to persuade their audiences of their supernatural abilities. These often involve stabbing oneself or piercing the body without shedding blood.

among the peoples they visited, but also the rituals and ceremonies that required instances of transgenderism. Despite this superficial act of cultural translation, ethnographic accounts reveal that shamans' sexuality is not reflected in their socially recognized gender. In fact, many transgender shamans are known to have married and fathered several children, as among the Taiwanese shamans known as *pulingaws*. It is, therefore, not possible to make general statements about the direct correlation between shamans' gender, sex and sexualities. The different combinations in which these elements come together clearly indicate that, in both theory and practice, shamans' bodies are different from those of ordinary humans.

Shamans' fluid identities reflect an inherent malleability of boundaries, not only between categories, but also between physical states. Most notably, this is reflected in the simultaneous porousness and impermeability of their bodies. It is said that shamans can both absorb substances and essences into their bodies, and expel them out. The ease with which they can project their souls out of themselves is testament to this ability. Yet, the opposite is equally true: shamans can seal the body so that nothing can penetrate the barrier of the flesh. Korean shamans demonstrate this impermeability by standing on a rack made of blades in bare feet without injury. There are many accounts among Siberian and Arctic practitioners, for example, of piercing, stabbing and cutting the skin without creating any bleeding or injury. Such feats are proof of the shaman's complete control over the physical world. It is the counterpart of the mastery they have over spirits and other incorporeal beings.

All that shamans do with their bodies promotes the idea that they are not ordinary humans, which indeed they are not. Defying the laws of physics and transcending normative categories are central to the practice of shamanism because, through the body, shamans demonstrate the legitimacy of doing shamanic work. The ability to shape-shift clearly illustrates this principle. Iban shamans from Sarawak, for example, are said to turn themselves into their

 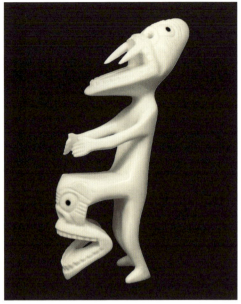

Tupilaq figure, Greenland
The variable appearance of tupilaqs is the result of the assemblage of different body parts into new beings created by evil shamans. Before having market appeal, tupilaqs had never been visually reproduced, because their horrific appearances struck terror in people.

neighbouring Malays, crossing ethnic boundaries in a way not possible for the other people in their communities. Also, shamans may blur the boundaries between species, becoming simultaneously an animal and a human. Stories of shape-shifting shamans abound. How they can achieve this may never be known, but the adoption of another species' outer form may be thought necessary in order to converse with that species, or to see the world from their perspective. Dark shamans may use this ability to turn into aggressive beasts to retaliate for a wrong experienced at the hands of enemies. Greenland shamans are said to be able to create monstrous beings called *tupilaq* by combining body parts from deceased animals and humans, using these creatures to carry out their orders to attack people.

Traversing domains of experience such as life and death, or the visible and the invisible, are equally proof of the shaman's extraordinary powers. The role of the 'psychopomp' (the one who conducts a dying person's soul to the land of the dead) is commonly carried out by shamans. While they may be bodily present in everyday reality assisting the moribund person, their spirit will accompany the recently deceased to the nether realms.

Carving of shaman during a seance, Alaska
The shaman is shown with his hands tied behind him, a practice that has also been recorded through photographs. Shamans can free themselves from ligatures and bindings using their power.

Shamans' bodies are demonstrably of a different nature from ordinary humans, they are believed to operate as easily in the high heavens as in the deep seas. They may withstand extreme conditions, including pain, sensory deprivation, fasting and long, exhausting ordeals as well as other difficult conditions, sometimes defying the laws of physics. It is said that in the past Inuit shamans would sit on an ice sheet in wet clothes and dry themselves simply by generating heat through concentration and willpower.

Alongside the ability to transform, shamans are usually endowed with second sight. They share this characteristic with spirit mediums, fortune-tellers, prophets and oracles, although shamans simultaneously perform many other roles. Second sight is directly linked to the visionary experiences that lie at the basis of shamanism everywhere. The capability to access inner, hidden or inaccessible areas of the mind, the body and the spirit worlds is essential to carry out

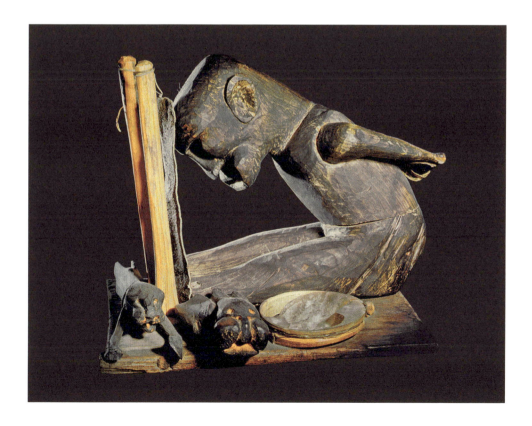

PROFILE TRANSFORMATION

This 900–300 BCE Olmec figurine from Mexico's Gulf Coast region is a composite anthropomorph. It combines human features with those of the jaguar, a central character in Olmec cosmology. Feline attributes are visible on the face and the feet appear to be turning into paws. The appearance of this hybrid creature encouraged some anthropologists to see in it the shamanic theme of transformation, an ability mustered by most shamans in the world.

OLMEC STATUE
This figurine (900–300 BCE) portrays a kneeling shaman in the act of transformation. At this point, he is shown to have both human and jaguar ears. In the Olmec culture, the kneeling position is associated with solemn ceremonies.

TLINGIT AMULET
Part-human, part-animal, this bone figurine displays features commonly linked with shamanism. The protruding tongue signifies spiritual power. Images of shamans receiving their power through kissing an animal are common in the Pacific Northwest.

COSTA RICAN STATUE
This 1000–1550 CE stone statue depicts a jaguar-man with a snake's tongue and relates to shamans' ability to shape-shift. This statue is among several found in Central America that likely would have been wedged into the ground so that they could stand.

HAIDA WOODEN STATUE
This Canadian figurine was made by the Haida artist Sdiihldaa/Simeon Stilthda (c. 1799–1889). It has been interpreted as a shaman in the act of transforming into a raven, an important bird in Haida oral traditions.

TAIRONA GOLD PECTORAL
Bats play a prominent role in Tairona shamanism from Colombia (900–1600 CE). Here, a shaman is depicted turning into a bat, as indicated by the upturned nose and fangs, typical of certain South American species.

SAN ROCK ART
Therianthropic (hybrid human–animal) figures appear in San rock art. In this rock painting from South Africa, the human body displays antelope hooves and an other-than-human face. San shamans can turn into elands and other animals.

197   THE MATERIAL WORLD —1— *The Body*

shamanic work. It is perhaps not surprising that some of the most powerful shamans and diviners recorded by ethnographers were blind. Their inward vision was considered to be a gift, one that other shamans can only attain artificially. For these others, seances are normally carried out in dimly lit or darkened places, with their eyes closed or covered. Fringes, scarves or blindfolds may be placed over their eyes to facilitate their inner vision and blot out the distractions of ordinary life.

Bodily techniques of this type are common throughout the shamanic world because they facilitate ASCs, which are an essential part of being a shaman. Shamans use a variety of methods to achieve the altered states that they need in order to perform their work with the intangible. Breathing, the use of rhythmical sounds, seclusion, fasting and sensory deprivation lead shamans to achieve visions, or to reach alternative registers of consciousness where they can interact with incorporeal beings and forces.

There is still much that modern scientists cannot explain about shamans' abilities, and sceptical minds are inclined to dismiss shamans' claims as mere fantasies. Yet, it is not uncommon to hear stories about ancient shamans' extraordinary aptitudes, which frequently translate into new generations' attempts at replicating past traditions. Even so, it can be argued that the decreasing time dedicated to shamanic training in many places often does not allow novices to develop and muster all the skills of their predecessors – perhaps including the ability to fly or to cut themselves without harm. Commercial ventures that promote one-size-fits-all apprenticeships rely on simple formulas that boil down a shaman's education to a few procedures, such as drumming or deep concentration; they leave out the many hard years of training and the dangerous tests that were once deemed essential to becoming a practitioner. Consequently, certain local knowledge about bodily techniques may have been neglected in the attempt at offering standard training. Clearly, these new versions of shamanism have radically altered the ways in which the shaman's body operates.

Waldemar Jochelson, Tungus man, Russia, 1901

Achieving inner vision is essential to shamans who spend long hours in sensory deprivation, often including closing or covering their eyes, in order to develop their skills of clairvoyance and divination. Looking inwards is not only useful for concentration, but also to refine one's sensory perception.

INSTRUMENTS

'[The ring] was placed on the drum, which was then beaten with the wand until the bouncing ring was finally stopped on some figure and refused to move away from it. The place where the ring had stopped revealed the will of the gods.'

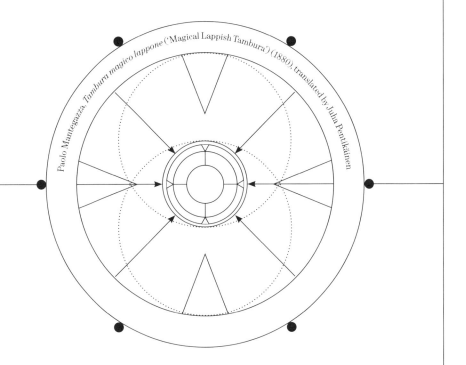

Paolo Mantegazza, *Tambura magico lappone* ('Magical Lappish Tambura') (1880), translated by Julia Pentikäinen

The great variety of objects used in shamanic practice shows cultural difference between shamanisms. These objects are technologies of the intangible that facilitate shamans' soul journeys, divination, healing and communication with invisible entities. The vibrant imagery they display reveals the richness and complexity of the shamanic universe and its inhabitants. The protection and aid they offer are essential to the practice of shamanism, which could not function without them.

Peoples without writing use different methods to communicate and transmit meanings in their societies. In a variety of social contexts, they may produce and use material and visual cultures, objects and images that encode – through colours, numbers, shapes and materials – what literate societies express through alphabets and writing. Among societies without written literature, artefacts and pictures variably convey ideas and concepts; human makers ingeniously assemble creative combinations that are based on specific codes and conventions determined by their own culture and tradition. The importance of these objects and pictures, therefore, lies not so much in their aesthetics, but in their level of significance as technologies of communication, archives of cultural knowledge and ritual tools. All this can be seen in the artefacts used and made by shamans around the world.

It is often said that shamans are the community's artists. This rings true if we consider that, in societies that do not separate people according to craft specialization, they are the only ones that manage, manipulate and transform cultural symbols into powerful artefacts. In much the same way as painters, writers and intellectuals do in societies with writing, shamans produce some of the most culturally significant expressions in their communities. Shamanic items that ordinary Western viewers may perceive as 'art' owing to their sculptural, painterly or communicative features are, in truth, inventive elaborations of concepts at the core of animistic lifeworlds. These objects are not created for pleasure, decoration or to be admired. Consequently the term 'art' may not fully capture their roles in the societies for which they were made. Objects and iconographies produced in shamanic contexts perform ritual and ceremonial functions, and are underpinned by animistic principles and ideas.

Shamanic material and visual cultures mirror the beliefs that shape, and are shaped by, the realities inhabited by the people that shamans serve. Each element of shamanic clothing and paraphernalia, and every ritual implement, is imbued with cosmological

⟨ *page 200*
Shaman drumming, Tuva, Russia
Percussion instruments are used almost universally in shamanic practice. Rhythmic beats help shamans reach a dissociative state that precedes the trance.

Renato Soares, Wauja man working on a mask, Mato Grosso, Brazil, 2019

The apapaatai that manifest in these masks are other-than-human beings that exist in the Wauja shamanic universe. Masks can be used as vessels for spirits and other entities that communicate with shamans.

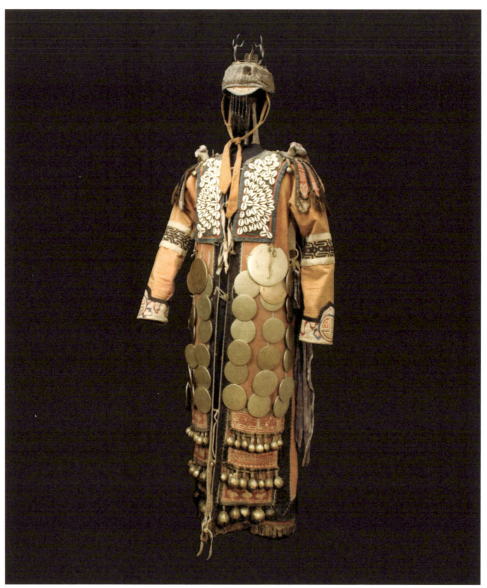

PROFILE
METALS AND
MINERALS

Minerals and metals' special qualities have been recognized since prehistory. Because these materials can be said to act or react – for example, they can change temperature, reflect light or generate sparks – agency is often attributed to them. Because of these powers, they are used to make special accoutrements, such as the discs on this Orochen shaman's coat, and tools that aid predictions, inflict injuries, deflect bad influences or heal.

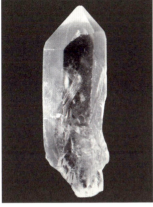

QUARTZ AND CRYSTALS
Qualities such as opalescence, transparency, reflectivity and thermoluminescence (emission of light from some minerals when they are heated) are taken to be a symptom of other-than-human agency. Minerals with these qualities are often incorporated into Neo-Shamanic practices.

COPPER
This *c.* 14th-century hammered copper depicts a double-headed falcon. Many pre-Columbian Indigenous North American peoples used this metal for the regalia of high-ranking shamans because it embodies the concept of transformation between states of being.

GREENSTONES
Like most Central American cultures, Costa Rican shamans used jade and other greenstones as aides in their ceremonies. Conceptualized as solidified water, it was employed to make shamanic jewelry that embodied exceptional power. This 1st–5th century CE jade pendant is from Nicoya, Costa Rica.

OBSIDIAN
Central American peoples associated obsidian with divination, prophecy and sacrifice. Among the Aztecs (1325–1521), who produced this mirror, it was the accessory of the shape-shifting god Tezcatlipoca, seen by some as a magician or a shaman-like figure.

GOLD
Chibcha shamans from Panama to Colombia appreciated gold alloyed with copper (*tumbaga*) because its colour was revealed by removing the first layer, a symbolic operation that stressed essence over appearance. This 400–900 CE gold-alloy pectoral was discovered at Sitio Conte.

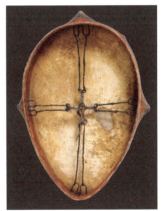

IRON
Iron is essential for Siberian shamans, who decorate their coats and fit their drums with it. For example, iron forms the handle at the back of this Evenk shamanic drum. Iron's longevity and strength are symbolically important because they signify durability and invincibility.

205   THE MATERIAL WORLD – 2 – *Instruments*

Shaman's fringed garment, Hulunbuir, Mongolia, 20th century
For the most part, fringes and streamers represent feathers and the shaman's ability to fly. In this case they represent snakes as shamanic helpers.

meanings, and is either related to iconographies associated with oral traditions and beliefs, or to things that exist in the animistic sensorium.

Figures, effigies and even what appear to be simple geometric motifs are more than mere symbols, from an animistic perspective. They are intentional agents in an extremely active and populated multiverse, one in which even the most nondescript-looking pendant may have power to protect, curse, attract, dazzle or deter. Shamanic implements and utensils are so powerful that they must be stored away from the community to avoid potential danger. No one can touch shamanic paraphernalia except the shaman. This is the reason why, when not directly confiscated during punitive campaigns against idolatry by colonial administrators, state officials and missionaries, most of the objects now in museum collections were recovered from funerary contexts, or found in secluded rock shelters and crevices or hidden in the woods.

Face carved on a *cong*, Liangzhu culture, China, 3200–2300 BCE
The figure carved on this cong (a type of Chinese ritual object) appears to be wearing a feather headdress that bears similarities to more recent specimens used by shamans in Siberia and Central Asia.

Among the oldest references to shamanic regalia are what have been interpreted as shamanic headdresses from the Liangzhu culture in China (3200–2300 BCE). The remarkable similarities in form between the figures etched on the mysterious Liangzhu ritual objects called *cong* and Central Asian shamans' feathered crowns suggest a long continuity between ancient and more modern cultures. Shamans from Tuva to Nepal still employ this type of headdress as an essential item of ritual regalia. Feathers are universally associated with birds and are used as a metaphor for flying, one of the many skills attributed to shamans. In Siberian shamanism, but also in subarctic North America, fringes may replace feathers and decorate large sections of the shaman's coat. A variation of the shaman's cloak is the human-hair cape of ancient Baja California, which enveloped the wearer from neck to calves. The highly decorated tunics worn by Siberian shamans facilitate contact with invisible dimensions; they are technologies of the incorporeal. There are numerous typologies of shamanic coats and tunics, varying by region. As might be expected, in warmer climates shamans do not wear coats, but they still have special accoutrements that are unique to their role and status.

DECODING SILLA CROWN

Korea's relationship with shamanism is very old, and the practice is still alive today. Shamanic ideas are reflected in the iconography of the royal crowns of the Silla Kingdom of Korea, as in this example that was excavated from the fifth-century Seobongchong tomb. Although it is not clear how the crowns were used in the context of royal ceremonialism, shamanic visual references are apparent. Similar headpieces are used among Siberian shamans, although they are usually made of iron rather than precious metals.

1.

COSMIC TREE
The central vertical motif found on all the known Silla crowns represents the cosmic tree, which connects all the levels of the universe. The tree referenced in this case may be the sacred tree that grew in the ritual precinct of Gyeongju, where this crown was entombed.

2.

SPANGLES
The discs hanging from the frame, branches and antlers may simply have had a functional purpose, but nonetheless they have a stunning visual impact. Their material was made using the same metallurgical technology as some Scythian specimens, which may prove Eurasian connections.

3.

ANTLERS
Antlers are common in shamanic crowns from Siberia. The shape of this crown's antlers likely references the reindeer, an important animal in North Asian beliefs, as it is often the mount used by shamans to start their spiritual journeys.

4.

JADE BEADS
The curved jade beads (*gogok*) hanging by thin, gold wire from the crown's vertical stems have been variably interpreted as visual metaphors: they may be fruits that symbolize fertility, canine teeth, half-moons or even, as some have suggested, human foetuses.

5.

GOLD
Cut from thin sheets of gold, the crown is very delicate and resembles specimens from the Afghan site of Tillya Tepe, and from Ukraine and Central Asia. The similarity between these gold objects suggests Scytho-Iranian influences via Siberia.

6.

SHAPE
The impractical shape of the crowns, and the fact that they were made from delicate gold, makes some scholars doubt that they were worn during ceremonies, suggesting that they were created solely as part of the mortuary kit for the Silla royal tombs.

209 THE MATERIAL WORLD — 2 — *Instruments*

Igu, Idu Mishmi people, Himalayan region, 2020

All eleven items of the igu's ritual regalia, known as amralapoh, *are protective. Only by wearing the* amralapoh *can these shamans receive the power they need to perform their duties as healers and ceremonialists. The igu's clothes and paraphernalia are not buried with him at his death in case a new shaman emerges in the future.*

Sashes and belts are used exclusively by shamans among the Apatani and the Idu Mishmi from the Himalayan region, and by Athapaskan and Inuit shamans in North America. Often these protective straps are decorated with miniature weapons that the practitioner may need during their spirit journeys.

Of utmost importance for Siberian shamans are mirrors, or alternatively round reflective plaques, that usually hang on the upper parts of the shaman's coat. Used since prehistory as divination tools, mirrors and reflective surfaces help shamans to see into the future, prophesy and even deflect the effects of enemy shamans' offensive powers. Reflective surfaces made of mica and pyrite have been found in ritual kits at archaeological sites belonging to several Native American cultures, such as the Hopewell (100–500 CE) and the Hohokam (300–1500 CE). It is still debated whether shamanism was established among these cultures. However, comparisons with Mexican societies developed after 900 CE (from which some of these tools are likely to have been imported) suggest at least a divinatory function. Divination and diagnosis in tropical South America and in the Antilles, but also in parts of Mexico, were/are conducted from special stools that align shamans to the cosmic axis that connects all the levels of the universe. Made of clay, volcanic stone, wicker or wood, the stools are seats of office and of power and are commonly used during the ingestion of psychotropic substances.

Most shamans' kits are not complete without special headdresses, or crowns, which are variably used by Amazonian, Korean and Pacific Northwest peoples, among others. Among the better known are the metal crowns of the Selkup and Evenk peoples from Siberia. These display antlers to which streamers are tied. Shamanic use of horns and antlers has been reported across the world and probably has ancient origins; even rock art figures may display headdresses, suggesting the diffusion of this item across time and space. Counterparts to these headdresses are the crowns employed by Tlingit, Tsimshian and Haida shamans from the Pacific Northwest. Made from

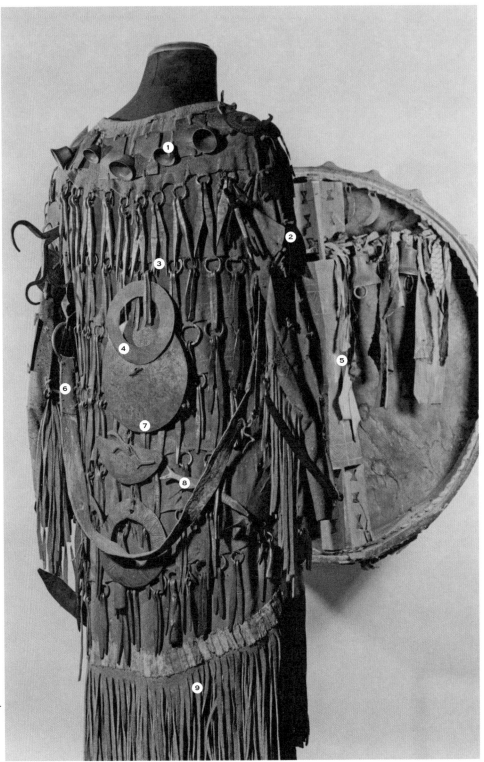

212 THE MATERIAL WORLD — 2 — *Instruments*

PROFILE
SIBERIAN SHAMAN'S COAT

Siberian shamans' coats are manifestations of the cosmos: the human body, the universe and animals are represented through painted symbols and trinkets hanging from the coats. Some of them incorporate pelts and hides from symbolic animals, and others are painted with colours associated with the moon, the sun, or night and day. Styles may change according to ethnic provenance, but all coats share some typical features.

1. BELLS
The clanging of bells and metal objects announce the shaman's arrival. They are also a way to scare evil spirits. The shaman's rhythmic bouncing and jumping creates music that accompanies drumming; these practices are used by shamans to achieve an ASCs. Hearing the sounds of the bells also helps the shaman to find their way back to earth.

2. METAL ARMOUR
Metal plates, stitched onto the sleeves and the front of the coat, function as armour while the shaman is in battle against spirits or evil opponents. At the front, they look like ribs and follow the rib cage's horizontal orientation. Skeleton imagery is also used by shamans to refer to their ability to see through skin.

3. METAL OBJECTS
Pointed, sharp and cutting metal objects frequently feature on shamans' coats as defence in case of incorporeal battles against evil forces. Some of these metal objects may have secret meanings known only to their owner. As such, they cannot be directly identified with anything found in this reality.

4. HOOP
This is an instrument that helps with the transition between realities. Holes, cracks in rocks, caves and springs may have the same function. They are portals for entering invisible dimensions. Sometimes, hoops are carved directly into a drum's handle. On coats, these hoops may be used to tie leather straps that are handled by the shaman's helpers.

5. DRUM FRAME
Several Siberian peoples build their drums by incorporating anthropomorphic figures in the frame. In this case, a human-like figure with outstretched arms functions as both a handle and a helper. This is where the shaman ties ribbon offerings to appease the helper, which in some cases is also the shaman's mount.

6. STRAP
The long, leather strap attached to the back of the coat is used to ensure that the shaman does not fall or injure himself or others during a seance. Straps such as this are handled by shamans' personal helpers, who make sure to prevent harm to both the practitioner and the public.

7. DISCS
Metal discs are very common in Central Asian and Siberian shamanism. They decorate shamans' coats, such as this one. Partially used as reflective, armoured surfaces that deflect evil blows, they are also the quintessential tool for divination. They function similarly to mirrors, which are used in other parts of the world to interpret the future.

8. ANIMAL EFFIGIES
A bird and a fish hang from the middle part of the coat's back, and more such animals are attached to the front. These are helpers that assist the shaman in flight and underwater. In some regions, shamans may add bear effigies or tigers, according to the different traditions that assign unique powers to specific animals.

9. FRINGES
This shaman's coat is heavily fringed. Fringes represent feathers that help shamans to fly to other dimensions. Among the Siberian Nganasan, fringes are also said to protect members of the community when they experience illness. In a coat with fringed sleeves, the shaman's arms offer shelter to their souls.

213   THE MATERIAL WORLD — 2 — *Instruments*

< Karol Schauer, artistic impression of the Bad Dürrenberg female shaman, 2004
This reconstruction is based on the artefacts recovered in Bad Dürrenberg in 1934, including the animal teeth and antlers shown to the right of the artwork.

> Animal teeth and antlers found during the excavations at Bad Dürrenberg, Germany, 7000–6800 BCE
This is what remains of an elaborate costume believed to be shamanic. The grave goods associated with this burial were covered in ochre, which is a clear sign of ritual use.

beaver incisors, or mountain-goat horn, they entirely encircle the head with upward-turned spikes.

Another important element of the Siberian shaman's outfit is the fringe that hangs from a headband or headdress used in seances. Acting as both a stimulant for entering an ASC and a screen against distractions from the ordinary world, shamanic facial fringes have become a common feature of the dress of Neo-Shamans and Neo-Pagan practitioners from Western countries. Indeed, it seems that dangling objects or fringes might also have been used by ritual practitioners in the European past, as testified in the reconstruction of what has been interpreted as a Mesolithic shamanic headpiece recovered by archaeologists in Bad Dürrenberg, Germany, in 1934.

Although not all shamans wear coats or headdresses like those of Siberian, Mongolian, Altaic and Turkic practitioners, they all employ musical instruments to accompany their sessions. Sounds, chants, refrains and echoes fill the shamanic soundscapes, and it is possible to say that shamanism is underpinned by a considerable acoustic component. Spirits and entities manifest

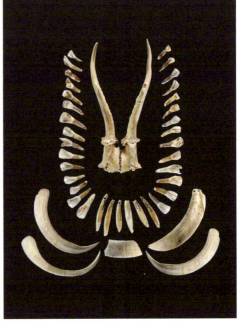

Mark Fox, Achuar shaman handling a *chakapa*, Ecuador, 2020
Rhythmically shaking the chakapa, *a leaf rattle, is meant to comfort the patient, cleanse their energies and trap the bad spirits in the bundle.*

themselves through unearthly sounds, and certain melodies or rhythms produced by humans enchant and hypnotize. It is no surprise that sounds and music play a central part in the multisensory world of shamanism. Sounds may also be a way to communicate with invisible entities. In fact, the clanging, rattling, banging and stomping of feet, hands and instruments may be used to clear malevolent beings from the space and to invite helpful entities into the rituals.

Kazakh shamans play stringed instruments such as the *kobyz*; Amazonian shamans use a variety of rattles, ocarinas and flutes; Indigenous California practitioners have clapping sticks; and the native Mapuche from Chile play bowl-shaped drums called *kultrun*. By and large, all the musical instruments used in shamanic practice are employed to produce entrancing rhythms that help the shaman reach an ASC.

The power of music to facilitate ASCs has also been recognized beyond shamanism. Whether religious or secular, the repetitive rhythms of certain music genres help listeners to enter alternative mental states and transcend ordinary reality. Similarities can be drawn,

François Guénet, Buryat female shaman, Mongolia, 2007
The hypnotic effect produced by drumming is as helpful to the shaman as it is for the patient, who is entranced, but to a lesser degree than the practitioner.

for example, between the immersive experience of a shamanic ecstatic trance and the secular experience of trance music at a rave, where repetitive rhythms characteristic of the trance genre are combined with substances including ecstasy and chemical mescaline.

Despite the diversity of instruments used in shamanic practice, in the Western imagination, drums have become the quintessential shamanic instrument. In recent years, their production – aimed at Neo-Shamans around the world – has skyrocketed. This is partially the result of the spread of Core Shamanic ideas endorsed by leading figures such as Michael Harner (1929–2018) and Jonathan Horwitz (born 1944), whose extremely popular workshops have drawn crowds all over the world. Practitioners are encouraged to personalize their drums, adopting symbols and designs from different places and making reference to various cultural origins. Traditional practitioners, by contrast, follow customary templates.

It is possible to determine a drum's origin from its shape and the figures that decorate it. A case in point

< **Saami drum from the Dutch edition of Johannes Schefferus's *Lapponia* (1682)**
The esoteric drawings on Saami drums triggered curiosity and apprehension in early voyagers. Thought to be associated with witchcraft and devil worship, these drums encapsulated the paganism that the voyagers sought to eradicate from Christian Scandinavia.

> **Saami shamanic drum, Saapmi, pre-1705**
This is one of the oldest surviving drums from the European Arctic. Rather than a mere musical instrument, the Saami's shamanic drums were technologies of supernatural communication.

are the Saami drums from Scandinavia. Once hundreds existed, but today only seventy remain in museum collections. Divided into three main classes according to regional typology, Saami drums display a limited variation in both shape and iconography. On the visible surface of drums from the north, one can identify the tripartite division of the cosmos into upper, middle and lower worlds. In the southern typology, the central sun (usually in the shape of a diamond) divides the painted field into four sections. Drums of the central region display a mix of the two. Saami drums were thus literal maps of the universe, in which humans, animals and other beings interacted via the shaman.

Not all shamanic drums are decorated in the same way. In fact, some may not be painted at all. In many cases, the back of the drum is more important than what the public can see. Indeed, drums' handles are where all the amulets and charms are hung. They are the closest to the shaman's body to shield them from harmful attacks. Siberian drums' handles may be carved in the shape of protecting figures or tutelary spirits, to which offerings are made, often in the

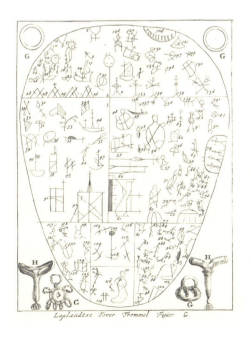

217   THE MATERIAL WORLD — 2 — *Instruments*

PROFILE
SHAMANIC
INSTRUMENTS

Shamans around the world employ a variety of instruments in their practice. Some objects are common to many different shamanic cultures, while others are completely unique to certain regions. Although drums appear to be the most widespread, there is a plethora of instruments – some musical and some not – that help shamans in areas such as achieving ASCs, healing, traversing the universe's many layers or combating evil forces. Below is a lavishly carved shamanic bowl from Brazil, which is at least 150 years old. Mortars and containers are used by shamans to pound and mix substances they use during their rituals, including, most notably, psychotropic agents that help shamans achieve ASCs. This vessel may have been used for this purpose.

SPATULA
This manatee-bone implement (900–1492 CE) was used by Taíno shamans of the Caribbean to induce vomiting. The practice was meant to purify oneself in preparation for the ingestion of cohoba, a psychotropic substance taken to achieve an ASC. Today, emetics are frequently used to cleanse the body before a seance.

STAFFS AND WANDS
Sticks, staffs and wands appear among the ritual paraphernalia of many shamans and shaman-like figures, including Viking seeresses, who used staffs such as these. They used distaffs (a tool for spinning) as their sign of office, a symbol of their connection to divination and fate, conceived of as a thread to be spun.

RATTLE
Rattles have been used in Native North and South American shamanic practice for centuries. Today, they are incorporated into the kits of many Neo-Shamanic practitioners who use instruments from a variety of different cultural sources, in line with the eclectic nature of their beliefs.

DRUM
The rhythmic beating of drums helps shamans to achieve ASCs. Most shamanic drums, including this Chilean Mapuche example, are hand-held. Inuit drums are the only ones that are beaten from below, due to the thinness of the frame. In some regions drums may be decorated with shamanic imagery.

MASK
Masks may be used by shamans in their rituals to communicate with different incorporeal beings. Masks similar to this c. 1800–1840 CE example, made by the Alaskan Tlingit, were used in healing rituals. The beings represented on these masks served as helpers for the shaman.

BOX
Shamans' storage boxes contained ceremonial paraphernalia and, sometimes, the shaman's urine, which was considered extremely powerful and was reportedly used by the shaman to wash themselves. Boxes were usually decorated with creatures meaningful to the owner. This Canadian Tlingit example dates from 1840–1850.

THE MATERIAL WORLD — 2 — *Instruments*

◁ **Haida soul catchers and pendant in the shape of the mythical sisiutl (bottom), Canada, 19th century**
Soul catchers are open on both sides to allow the shaman to suck and trap diseases or to blow an escaped soul back into the body. The imagery of soul catchers relates to shape-shifting and includes representations of animals that mediate between realms, water, air and land.

▷ **Snuff tube, Brazil, pre-15th century**
This object, used to inhale pulverized psychotropic plants, shows an animal towering over a human. The animal's power is transmitted to the inhaling person when the substance passes through the tube.

form of ribbons and strips of cloth. The handle is also frequently compared to a bow that shoots the shaman into other dimensions. In some cases, the handle may have a narrow opening through which the practitioner may enter invisible registers of reality.

Owing to the extreme variety of practices and beliefs, shamanic kits may include instruments that are unique to certain regions. Exclusive to North American shamanisms, practised from Baja California to Alaska, are the so-called sucking tubes. Variably made of stone, bone, reeds or clay, these seemingly unassuming implements are extremely important in shamans' healing practices. Sucking tubes are cylindrical and have openings on both sides. They can be decorated or plain and may be used for both smoking and curing. Because of the therapeutic functions associated with tobacco among several Indigenous American peoples, and the belief that diseases are caused by spirit theft, inhaling and exhaling stand for the action needed to extract a malignant agent from the ailing body, and to restore a wandering spirit to the diseased person by blowing it back into the body.

Ceremonial *metate*, Costa Rica, *c.* 100–500 CE
The underside of this grindstone shows a transforming shaman. The object may have been used to grind sacred plants for rituals.

In most cases, the historic use of cactuses, seeds, flowers, mushrooms or vines for shamanism necessitated the production of a separate inventory of implements and utensils. The Scythians (seventh–third century BCE) of Central Asia, who burned cannabis seeds to inhale the smoke, left cauldrons that were used for this purpose during steam baths. Yet, in places such as Siberia where the use of mushrooms has been recorded, no implement directly related to their consumption has been positively associated with the practice.

The situation is different in the Americas, particularly in regions such as the Caribbean, Ecuador, Argentina, Chile and the Peruvian Andes, where archaeological excavations have recovered complex and rich sets of implements produced solely for the consumption of psychoactive plants or mushrooms. The remarkable snuff tablets and inhalers found throughout the Antilles and South America show extraordinary similarities in their functionalities and use. Typically, the imagery associated with this practice relates to felines, or to shamans who are in

221   THE MATERIAL WORLD — 2 — *Instruments*

the process of transforming, or who hold ceremonial tools. Sacred animals or mythological characters may be depicted on trays, grindstones and stools employed by shamans at different stages of the ceremonials. On the Pacific Northwest coast, for instance, like in northern Peru, mortars and pestles were used to mash herbs, roots, berries and plants used in ancient rituals of a shamanic nature. This is testified by a remarkably continuous iconography including figures associated with shamans, for example, the representation of frogs or felines.

A less frequent, yet important theme in shamanic accoutrements is that of the shaman's double. Many Indigenous American societies maintain that each person is associated with an animal at birth. For shamans these are tutelary animals that transmit their powers to the shaman. In the case of the pre-15th century Brazilian snuff tube shown on page 220, the shaman who inhaled psychotropic powders through the cavity was believed to receive the protective powers of the animal represented in the carved effigy on the inhaler.

Modern shamanisms use far fewer implements and utensils, and a great deal of related knowledge has been lost due to cultural changes, religious conversion and the lack of apprentices. Masks, which once were part of the shamanic kit of several societies from Siberia to the Pacific Northwest, are now only curious artefacts in museum collections. Yet many objects continue to perform their customary role in rites, ceremonies and offerings. Libation spoons, staffs and whips are used by many tribal peoples in the forests of Malaysia, Yunnan, the Himalayas and the Amazon. The continuous reworking of traditional repertoires by nativistic movements greatly reshaped shamanic toolkits. This is particularly noticeable in the integration of different religious traditions with Neo-Shamanic practices, which in some quarters may include an unprecedented mix of Tibetan singing bowls, Himalayan bells, runic stones, crystals and ceremonial staffs not commonly associated with the practice of shamanism.

Shaman at the Narayanthan Jatra festival, Tamal, Nepal

Drums, bells, wooden daggers, flutes, portable altars and chest armour are commonly used by Nepalese shamans. Peacock feathers were sent by the Cosmic Mother to the shamans to make bonnets, such as the one worn here, that act as bridges to the spirit world.

223   THE MATERIAL WORLD — 2 — *Instruments*

PLACES AND SPACES

'Finally, he comes to the place of the soul's captivity, where he
gives a shout of triumph and begins to bargain with the gods of the
underworld, imploring them to free the soul. Finally, with the soul
in his possession, the shaman returns by the same route.'

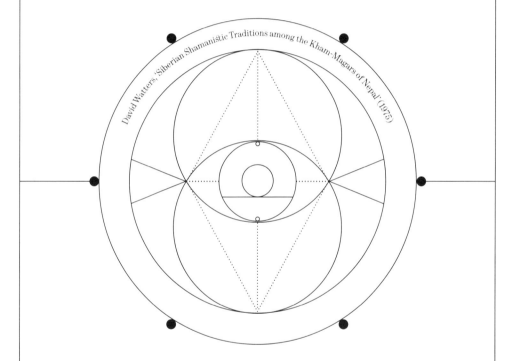

David Watters, 'Siberian Shamanistic Traditions among the Kham-Magars of Nepal' (1975)

Shamans live in animated geographies that comprise visible
and invisible places, which they visit in both corporeal and incorporeal
forms. Sites of pilgrimage, worship and ceremony create a spiritual network
that connects ordinary people and shamans to other-than-human beings
through prayers, invocations, rituals and sacrifices. Whether located
in faraway places or in the comfort of one's home, these powerful
sites are central to shamanic activity.

The notion that nature is a neutral space, requiring human intervention to turn it into a meaningful place, is profoundly alien to shamanistic worldviews. From the animistic perspective adopted by shamans around the world, there is no space in this reality that is ever empty, even where there appears to be no sign of human life. The universe is made up of different connecting layers, and the inhabitants of each one live in parallel dimensions; they can only see or experience the other layers under very specific circumstances. Arawakan peoples from Peru, for example, know that the landscape they occupy is also dotted with invisible houses where the spirits live; humans may never see them, except in dreams.

To animists, meaningful landscapes pre-date human presence because other-than-human persons dwell everywhere. Geographical features are peopled by invisible entities, spirits, ancestors, demons and other elusive presences, with whom humans must share this world and negotiate the terms of their coexistence. Shamans make sure that the parts of the physical world that they occupy can be turned into places where they, and the communities they look after, can carry out ritual and ceremonial activities to acknowledge these relationships with invisible beings and the sites they inhabit. Such places may be cemeteries, sanctuaries, stations for meditation and seclusion, or places of pilgrimage.

Acknowledging that different degrees of spiritual activity are present in the landscape is central to shamanism. Mountains, rock shelters, caves, crossroads, islands, boulders, rivers, springs, lakes and even constellations come to be regarded as sacred owing to their exceptional power, or sometimes to their unusual morphology. The latter may be explained as the result of ancient heroes and the heroic actions of powerful shamans or their helpers. For example, the Mansi people of West Siberia claim that when their ancestral hero Moś chased the cosmic elk, his footsteps were left as stars in the sky. Perhaps the best-known example is Nanabozho, a shape-shifting trickster, shaman and creator among the Algonquian

< *page 224*
Statue of shaman with scarf offerings, Mongolia, 2019
In Central Asia, marking space with permanent monuments has been practised since antiquity. Today, realistic statues mark special places, like memorial steles and gravestone pillars did in the past.

Poles with scarf offerings on Shaman Rock, Olkhon Island, Lake Baikal, Russia, 2019

These poles represent the thirteen celestial beings that descended from the sky to judge human actions. Derived from horses' tethering poles, they also symbolize the tree of life or the cosmic tree. The colours of the ribbons and scarves left as offerings have different purposes: white for health and blue for other wishes, for instance.

Sleeping Giant, Ontario, Canada
Anishinaabe people identify this mountain with the shape-shifting Nanabozho, an important character from their oral traditions.

peoples of eastern Canada. After creating the world, Nanabozho rested by the shore of Lake Superior near Sault Ste. Marie, and the shape of his sleeping body is still visible today in the form of a rocky outcrop.

Quite frequently, these natural features are seen as literal manifestations of incorporeal beings. Among the Nanai (or Goldi) in eastern Siberia, the Amur River is believed to be the living body of the dragon Puymur, the essence of water. Owing to the intensity of the perceived divine presence, such places as the double-headed boulder Sŏnbawi become powerful initiation sites for Korean shamans and in addition can grant fertility. Equally important are certain rock formations found in Peru's Amazonian jungle. There, southern Arawakan peoples such as the Yanesha and Ashaninka leave offerings of coca leaves to what they believe are spirits turned to stone at the beginning of time.

Selected spots in the landscape may also become the focus of shamanic activity because they facilitate communication between cosmic levels, or are seen as portals to other-than-human dimensions. In the Siberian region of Khakassia, as in Indigenous California, natural features such as cracks in rocky walls and narrow passages between large stones are considered to be doors into other dimensions. Iconography associated

San rock art, Bushmans Kloof, South Africa, 2007
Figures with elongated arms suggest shamanic activity at this site. Some locations were selected because of their inherent power.

with shamanism appears at these sites, and oral traditions corroborate their shamanic character.

These sacred geographies draw the boundaries of distinctive shamanic traditions celebrated in oral traditions and customary practice, and the artefacts and visual expressions found there are typically interpreted according to the traditions common in those regions. This is particularly true for rock art, which displays significant stylistic and iconographic diversity, and which can be deciphered only by those who know the myths and rituals performed by local shamans, a role sometimes taken by present-day Indigenous specialists who can 'read' ancient rock art.

In southern Africa, scenes of shamanic rituals are depicted realistically. Vignettes representing seances show practitioners bleeding from the nose or curing the sick, or even instances of human–animal transformation. In other parts of the world, geometric designs may interact with naturalistic figures, for example in Finland where human limbs extend into snakes, or in Canada's Peterborough petroglyphs, where stars and other celestial bodies form part of the human anatomy. In other cases, walls are completely covered in abstract forms and shapes. While the cultural significance of

PROFILE
SACRED PLACES

Shamanic landscapes are filled with sacred places that are either related to the oral traditions of certain populations or are sites dedicated to shamanic activities. These places may be portals to other dimensions, sites of communication between realities, or stations for meditation, training or initiation. Caves, boulders, rock shelters, mountain peaks, rivers or lakes where particular spirits or entities reside are the most common sacred places from a shamanic perspective, but personal altars or consecrated areas of domestic space that are used for rituals or ceremonies qualify too.

PANTHER CAVE, TEXAS, USA
On the bank of the Seminole Canyon, this important site features massive wall paintings of shamans and their journeys into the spirit world, as well as a leaping cat. The paintings are dated to *c.* 7000 BCE–600 CE. The shelter may have been used for ritual activities and initiation rites managed by shamans of the Lower Pecos.

DRAKENSBERG TRANSFORMING SHAMANS, SOUTH AFRICA
Informants local to the Drakensberg mountains reveal that the rock art sites there were places where people would congregate to receive the spiritual potency emitted by the images. Like in many other regions, site choice was as important as the images painted on the rocky surfaces.

SHAMAN ROCK, OLKHON ISLAND, LAKE BAIKAL, RUSSIA
Buryats believe that Azin, the guardian of the Shaman Rock, resides inside the rock itself. Rocks, mountains and boulders are animate beings in Siberian cultures. This important sacred site attracts shamans from all over Siberia who come here to pay homage to the powerful spirits that inhabit the lake and the rock.

WIRIKUTA MOUNTAIN, SAN LUIS POTOSÍ, MEXICO
Sacred to the Huichol people who make yearly pilgrimages to the site, this mountain and the desert that surrounds it are considered to be the place of origin for all people. This site is also where peyote ceremonies take place, under the supervision of a shaman.

TAMGALY VALLEY, KAZAKHSTAN
This cultic site displays thousands of petroglyphs, hundreds of which are shamanic in nature. In addition to the recognizable shamanic figures, there are images of horses, many of which are split in two by apertures in the rocks. These cracks are portals that are used by shamans on horseback to travel inside the mountain.

GREAT SALBYK BURIAL MOUND, KHAKASSIA, RUSSIA
A massive, phallic stone monument towers over a burial. Like other similar standing stones, it has links to shamanism, here confirmed by the offerings left by local people. Though not a pilgrimage site per se, stones are considered living beings that protect and ensure good health or, sometimes, fertility.

231   THE MATERIAL WORLD — 3 — *Places and Spaces*

Serranía de la Lindosa rock shelter, Colombia, 2016
This shelter has been used since around 10,000 BCE. The painted panel shown here includes geometric designs similar to entoptics, as shown on page 171. Their meaning is unknown.

these visual expressions undoubtedly lies within the meanings embedded in the motifs, the location of rock art panels is no less relevant. Rock art is usually positioned at strategic points in the landscape, typically at sites where rituals and ceremonies take place, or where shamans retreat for long periods of seclusion and training. Such places are selected due to their spiritual importance and because they are considered to be densely populated by other-than-human beings, with whom shamans forge lasting relationships. At these sites, depictions of dreams and visions may be more frequent than realistic imagery with narrative content. Sites marked by petroglyphs (rock carvings) may be particularly sacred to local populations, who may either revere them or avoid them altogether. In some cases, such visual representations are purposely placed in hard-to-reach places, whether deep in the jungle, inside caves or on remote rocky outcrops.

Indigenous representations of shamans or their accoutrements are ubiquitous in shamanic landscapes, from Scandinavia to Siberia, in Mongolia, China, southern Africa and the Americas. Though stylistically some of these pictures may be rather schematic, it is

Cave of Arrows, Baja California, Mexico, 15,000–6000 BCE
Jesuit missionary records describe shaman headdresses in this area. One of many regional variations is depicted here.

possible to detect in them elements directly related to shamanic practices and beliefs. Psychotropic plants used in ASCs regularly appear in rock art, as do drums, cloaks and headdresses, among other items. In a rather small region of Mexico's Baja California, for example, more than a dozen shamanic headdresses have been spotted, several of which correspond to descriptions left by eighteenth-century Jesuit missionaries and other eyewitnesses. Each of these may belong to a particular area controlled by a shaman, identified by the distinctive accoutrements they used. In the same way, the extremely detailed representations of drums found in Siberian rock art reveal the cultural significance of this ritual object in shamanic ceremonialism, and also indicate distinctive local traditions operating in particular areas at different points in time.

Powerful places are classified differently in shamanic landscapes according to the use that humans make of them. They can be divided into communal or private spaces, or sites only accessible by shamans

Tenon heads, Chavín de Huántar, Ancash, Peru, 1200–400 BCE
These sculptures are two of the one hundred stone heads that once decorated the outer walls of the main temple at Chavín de Huántar. Only one remains in place today. On the left, the shaman's head is depicted in the process of transforming into a jaguar. The final sculpture of the cycle, shown on the right, depicts the final stage of the shaman's transformation.

and consequently forbidden to the general population. Communal areas may be accessed freely, or visits may be permitted only at specific times of the year, for example during events, ceremonies or special rituals in which shamans have a central role. Some of these places may become the focus of pilgrimages: for example, Real de Catorce in the state of San Luis Potosí in Mexico, where lies Wirikuta, the sacred desert of the Huichol people; or the site of the Blythe geoglyphs made by Yuman tribes in southern California, which depict the creator deity Mastamho and his dog.

These pilgrimage sites may also be associated with prophetic activities and divination, as in the case of the ancient site of Chavín de Huántar. Situated at the foot of Peru's northern Andes, at the intersection of two major rivers, this megalithic centre was at once a temple, an oracle and a centre of pilgrimage between 1200 and 400 BCE. The inner chambers of the main structure housed the *Lanzón* (Spanish for 'big spear'), a stone stele that spoke through the voices of shaman-priests under the influence of a psychotropic plant. Probably this plant was the San Pedro cactus, which is shown being handled by figures in relief sculptures at the same site. One hundred stone heads once adorned the outer walls of the main temple, showing the different phases of a shaman transforming into a jaguar, including mucus discharging from the nostrils, a common effect of the ingestion of psychotropic agents.

Feng Qu, *ominan* ritual, China, 2020
Daur people stage this ritual every three years. The ceremonial grounds are usually staged near a river, depending on the spirits' instructions.

Roads and paths connecting sacred sites can often be identified by the deposition of offerings at particular junctions. These can be found in places such as cemeteries or shrines, or at natural features, creating an invisible network of shamanic geographies. Leaving small gifts at selected sites serves the purpose of befriending the entities that inhabit those places. Making the offering may require a particular demeanour, speaking in a low voice, or acknowledging the beings with short prayers or invocations. Libations, such as milk or alcohol, may be poured at specially made shrines. In Mongolia these are called *ovoos*, and are cairns, or mounds made of stones piled up by worshippers. They are topped by carved poles around which hundreds of ribbons, strips of cloth and food or drink are left as offerings. Important among these objects are the blue silk scarves called *khadag* left in honour of Tengri, the sky. Like other pilgrimage sites, these high-altitude cairns, often placed at the intersection of rivers or crossroads, are regularly visited and acknowledged by ordinary people and shamans alike.

While ordinary people may feel compelled to frequent particular sites because of the power that

DECODING DEER STONES

Between 1200 and 700 BCE, nomadic peoples crossing the Central Asian plains began erecting stone monuments in areas around Lake Baikal, the Yenisei River and the Altai mountains. Steles found in these regions are replete with symbolism that scholars have associated with shamanic ideas and material culture. While only a portion of them display detectable human faces, their bodies are undeniably anthropomorphic. Represented on them are implements that are used by shamans, and even the body markings they feature indicate shamanic imagery.

FACE
Human-like faces on deer stones are carved in the round. The sides sometimes show earrings. The typical pursed lips have been interpreted as the act of singing, proclaiming or invoking spirits, as if during a shamanic seance.

TATTOOS
The steles are often covered in markings that are reminiscent of the tattoos of Scythian mummies found in Siberia. Supporting a shamanic reading of the imagery is the presence of rib cage motifs, which recur on shamanic items.

HORSE SACRIFICE
Several steles are linked with horse sacrifice, possibly as offerings or as ritual killings for a person commemorated by the stone. Horses in shamanic contexts are often messengers, possibly tying these stones to shamanic themes.

MIRRORS
Circular motifs above the central band encircling the stele's body may represent mirrors. Mirrors are common shamanic divination and ritual tools that can be found in the toolkit of diviners from Mexico to China.

BELTS AND WEAPONS
Belts and miniature weapons are commonly used by shamans to fight evil forces and marked on some deer stones. Belts and sashes are part of the inventory of shamans in the Himalayas, Arctic and Bering Sea areas.

DEER
The animal that gives its name to this type of monument has strong shamanic associations and appears on many steles. Its leaping motion suggests flight towards the sky or perhaps the sun, which is also visible in some deer stones.

237   THE MATERIAL WORLD — 3 — *Places and Spaces*

Tlingit shaman's grave, Alaska, 19th century
In the Pacific Northwest shamans were usually buried in special graveyards and given grave 'houses' to be used in the afterlife.

they emit, there are other places that are decidedly off limits owing to the exceptional risk they may pose to visitors and even to passers-by. Shamans' graves, cemeteries and tombs may be particularly unsafe due to the high levels of spiritual activity that take place there. Any individual unable to manage other-than-human interaction may be in great danger.

Shamans' resting places are the culmination of often long and complex travels undertaken by souls to reach the land of the dead. Sometimes ghosts linger around the house, waiting to be accompanied to their final destination, as Himalayan Idu Mishmi tribals believe. Shamans who have the role of psychopomps must follow tortuous paths to the world of the dead, which starts with visualizing the actual places where the journey begins. Vivid accounts of the lands of ghosts, the dead or ancestors reveal the spirit worlds' elaborate cartographies. Several Siberian and American peoples describe rivers of tears, or the Milky Way, as the expressway to the land of the dead. Arawakan shamans in the process of retrieving their patients' lost souls systematically name all the places they visit in

Archaeological excavations at a burial mound, Kazakhstan
Central Asian burial mounds (kurgans) are considered protectors of the land. They are respected living entities with which humans entertain relationships of reciprocity.

the metaphysical realm. Rare representations of some of these places have been drawn by shamans after their safe return to the land of the living.

Despite the great attention paid to the physical world, in shamanic thinking not all spaces are visible, and some may exist without geographical coordinates. Individual shamans may visualize them in their mind's eye to travel there in incorporeal form. Sometimes, instead of a specific site, concrete visualizations are used for cosmic travel. Yakut shamans from Siberia, for example, travel between worlds using large metal rings that they pin to their ceremonial coats. Inuit shamans use the holes that appear in their masks for similar purposes. Space, in shamanic thought, is both physical and transcendent, and this interconnection reflects the principle that what is visible to the eye has its corresponding double in the metaphysical realm. Animals or plants are corporeal forms of spirits, and other-than-human beings can be met in incorporeal form; the same is true of space. For example, tents' smoke holes may be convenient metaphors to visualize entrances to and exits from cosmic realms.

What Westerners call 'nature' or 'landscape' is essential to the creation of sacred geographies.

DECODING CONTEMPORARY MESA ALTAR

The incorporation of eclectic elements from different cultural traditions is typical of contemporary Western shamanism. Andean traditions preserved by the Peruvian ritual specialists called Q'eros are among the many customs that have been integrated into different strands of Core Shamanism. Though Q'eros have never claimed to be shamans, their ancient knowledge resonates with some of the principles that

1. CANDLES
Derived from European traditions, candles were imported into the Americas by Spanish and Portuguese Catholics. They are now part of Indigenous rituals in many parts of the Americas, carrying elements of the Christian faith into local ritual practices. These are syncretic religions.

2. STONES
The inclusion of stones, and sometimes shells, in *mesa* altars is a custom derived from Andean cosmology, which gives agency to rocks and mountains. Collected over time and from different geographical regions, *mesa* pebbles symbolize different environments, such as the sea or the mountains.

3. WRAPPINGS
Andean textiles are essential to wrap all the items that constitute the portable altar. They usually bear symbols of the mountains and other natural elements that relate to the cardinal directions (north, south, east and west) or the cosmic regions, such as the sky, the earth and the lower regions.

4. CRYSTALS
Usually associated with chakras and energy points, crystals may be included in *mesa* wrappings as a reference to some Indigenous American traditions and Eastern philosophies, adding a sense of globalization to what is an entirely local tradition. Some Amerindian traditions use crystals for divination.

5. PERSONAL CHARMS
Personal bundles may be common among some Native societies, where they are used to guard ritual objects relevant to the owner, but in *mesa* altars following Core Shamanism, objects and charms with personal meaning reflect a belief in the cross-cultural equivalence of symbols and their power.

6. TAROT CARDS
Clearly imported from European tradition, divination cards can be seen as a substitute for the coca leaves commonly used in the Andes for fortune-telling. The syncretic nature of object combinations in contemporary *mesas* testifies to the syncretic nature of Core Shamanism.

underpin Core Shamanism and New Age movements. The mixing of Western shamanism with the customs of the Q'eros is visible in the contemporary *mesa* (portable shrine) below. Objects from distant places are brought together in the *mesa* that, though broadly inspired by ancient Peruvian knowledge, provide a direct and individualized link to the modern practitioner's personal experience.

Consequently, landscapes are prominent in shamanic practices and oral traditions. Yet, equally important to shamans are the distinct areas within the built environment dedicated to ritual and ceremonial activities. Tents such as chums, yarangas, gurs and yurts, but also longhouses or even modern apartments, may contain areas devoted to storing shamanic accoutrements, or may accommodate certain ritual activities. Some of them may have altars and shrines dedicated to ancestors or deceased shamans, or sections for divination and for healing sessions. Home shrines and performance areas are central to the Korean *mansin*. Purposefully dressed altars house incense, offerings, candles and commercial objects that indicate a *mansin*'s relative degree of success with her tutelary spirits and helpers. Above the altar hang images of the gods and deceased shamans met by the altar's owner in dreams and visions. They serve as a temporary home for the beings who are regularly called into the room to help the *mansin* with her shamanic work.

The revival of shamanism over the last few decades has progressively moved shamanic activities into the home, especially among shamans who practise in urban centres. Altars and shrines have begun to function as individual practitioners' own ritual areas, carved out of ordinary domestic spaces. Healing sessions, chanting, ayahuasca ceremonies and, not infrequently, highly elaborate ceremonies may be conducted privately indoors, given the stigma and regulations often associated with shamanism and its most common practices. On the other hand, sacred traditional cartographies have also been enriched with new places as an effect of the commercialization of shamanism in many countries. Such sites as Lake Baikal, or mountains such as Kihiléékh in the Sakha Republic (Yakutia), have been rebranded as healing sites as part of astute marketing campaigns aimed at developing tourism in these regions. Though some of these sites may have been sacred to local groups before the popularization of shamanism, the extent to which they attract tourists from around the world is unprecedented and will likely continue into the foreseeable future.

> *pages 244–45*
> Shaman's shrine,
> Taklamakan Desert,
> China, 2007
> *Ribbons, flags and offerings indicate that this is an active, regularly visited site. Some shamans are greatly revered due to their reputations as powerful healers, and their memory continues for generations.*

Jorge Mañes Rubio, shaman carries out a public ritual, Namhansanseong Mountain, Korea, 2017

Korean shamans frequently act in specially prepared spaces that accommodate for the participation of spirits and other entities. Fitted with altars for offerings, they are surrounded by living effigies inhabited by old shamans and deities. Domestic interiors are suitable for private rituals.

FURTHER READING

SOURCES OF QUOTATIONS

9 *Historia Norwegie*, eds Inga Ekrem and Lars Boje Mortensen, trans. Peter Fisher (Copenhagen: Museum Tusculanum Press, 2003 [12th century]), p. 61

39 Quoted in: Lumholtz, Carl, *Unknown Mexico*, Vol. I (New York: Charles Scribner's Sons, 1902), p. 516

63 Quoted in: Kara, Dávid Somfai, 'Rediscovered Kumandy Shamanic Texts in Vilmos Diószegi's Manuscript Legacy', *Shaman*, Vol. XXVI, Nos. 1–2 (2018), pp. 107–32; p. 124

87 Kamenskii, Anatolii, *Tlingit Indians of Alaska*, trans. and ed. Sergei Kan (Fairbanks, AK: University of Alaska Press, 1985 [1906]), pp. 85–86

111 Quoted in: Holmer, Nils, and Henry Wassén, 'The Complete Mu-Igala in Picture Writing', *Etnologiska Studier*, Vol. XXI (1953), pp. 1–158

131 Bell, John, *Travels from St Petersburg in Russia to Diverse Parts of Asia*, Vol. I (Glasgow: Robert and Andrew Foulis, 1763 [1720]), pp. 206–7

155 Boas, Franz, 'Tsimshian Mythology', based on texts recorded by Henry Wellington Tate, *Thirty-First Annual Report of the Bureau of American Ethnology 1909–1920* (Washington, DC: Government Printing Office, 1916), pp. 27–1037; p. 384

179 Bogoras, Waldemar, *The Chuckchee*, Part 2: Religion, *Memoirs of the American Museum of Natural History*, Vol. XI (Leiden: E. J. Brill Ltd, 1904), p. 449

201 Quoted in: Pentikäinen, Juha, 'The Shamanic Drum as Cognitive Map', *Cahiers de littérature orale*, No. 67–8 (2010), pp. 1–12; pp. 4–5

225 Watters, David, 'Siberian Shamanistic Traditions among the Kham-Magars of Nepal', *Contributions to Nepalese Studies*, Vol. II, No. 1 (1975), pp. 123–68; p. 147

GENERAL

Alberts, Thomas Karl, *Shamanism, Discourse, Modernity* (London: Routledge, 2015)

Djaltchinova-Malec, Elvira Eevr (ed.), *Shamanhood and Art* (Budapest: Akadémiai Kiadó, 2014)

DuBois, Thomas, *An Introduction to Shamanism* (Cambridge: Cambridge University Press, 2009)

Eliade, Mircea, *Shamanism: Archaic Techniques of Ecstasy* (Princeton, NJ: Princeton University Press, 1964)

Flaherty, Gloria, *Shamanism and the Eighteenth Century* (Princeton, NJ: Princeton University Press, 1992)

Francfort, Henri-Paul, and Roberte N. Hamayon (eds), *The Concept of Shamanism: Uses and Abuses* (Budapest: Akadémiai Kiadó, 2001)

Furst, Peter T., *Flesh of the Gods: The Ritual Use of Hallucinogens* (Long Grove, IL: Waveland Press, 1990)

Halifax, Joan, *Shaman: The Wounded Healer* (London: Thames & Hudson, 1982)

Harvey, Graham (ed.), *Shamanism: A Reader* (London: Routledge, 2002)

Harvey, Graham, and Robert J. Wallis, *Historical Dictionary of Shamanism* (Lanham, MD: Rowman & Littlefield, 2015)

Hultkrantz, Åke, *Shamanic Healing and Ritual Drama* (New York: Crossroad, 1992)

Hutton, Ronald, *Shamans: Siberian Spirituality and the Western Imagination* (London: Hambledon Continuum, 2007)

Jacobsen, Merete Demant, *Shamanism: Traditional and Contemporary Approaches to the Mastery of Spirits and Healing* (New York: Berghahn, 2020)

Kehoe, Alice Beck, *Shamans and Religion: an Anthropological Exploration in Critical Thinking* (Long Grove, IL: Waveland Press, 2000)

Lewis, Ian, *Ecstatic Religion: A Study of Shamanism and Spirit Possession*, 3rd edn (Abingdon: Routledge, 2003)

Löben Sels, Robin van, *Shamanic Dimensions of Psychotherapy: Healing through the Symbolic Process* (Abingdon: Routledge, 2019)

Narby, Jeremy, and Francis Huxley (eds), *Shamans Through Time: 500 Years on the Path to Knowledge* (London: Thames & Hudson, 2001)

Price, Neil (ed.), *The Archaeology of Shamanism* (London: Routledge, 2001)

Ripinsky-Naxon, Michael, *The Nature of Shamanism: Substance and Function of a Religious Metaphor* (Albany, NY: State University of New York Press, 1993)

Thomas, Nicholas, and Caroline Humphreys (eds), *Shamanism, History and the State* (Ann Arbor, MI: University of Michigan Press, 1996)

Thorpe, S. A., *Shamans, Medicine Men and Traditional Healers: A Comparative Study in Shamanism in Siberian Asia, Southern Africa and North America* (Pretoria: UNISA Press, 1993)

Tomášková, Silvia, *Wayward Shamans: The Prehistory of an Idea* (Berkeley, CA: University of California Press, 2013)

Vitebsky, Piers, *Shamanism* (Norman, OK: University of Oklahoma Press, 2001)

Wallis, Robert J., and Max Carocci (eds), *Art, Shamanism and Animism* (Basel: MDPI Press, 2022)

Williams, Mike, *Prehistoric Belief: Shamans, Trance and the Afterlife* (Stroud: The History Press, 2010)

Winkelman, Michael J., *Shamanism: A Biopsychosocial Paradigm of Consciousness and Healing* (Santa Barbara, CA: Praeger, 2010)

Yamanda, Takako, and Mihály Hoppál (eds), *An Anthropology of Animism and Shamanism* (Budapest: Akadémiai Kiadó, 2000)

Znamenski, Andrei A., *The Beauty of the Primitive: Shamanism and the Western Imagination* (Oxford: Oxford University Press, 2007)

ASIA

Anawalt, Patricia Rieff, *Shamanic Regalia in the Far North* (London: Thames & Hudson, 2014)

Balzer, Marjorie Mandelstam (ed.), *Shamanic Worlds: Rituals and Lore of Siberia and Central Asia* (Abingdon: Routledge, 2017)

Balzer, Marjorie Mandelstam (ed.), *Shamanism: Soviet Studies of Traditional Religion in Siberia and Central Asia* (London: M. E. Sharpe, 1990)

Buyandelger, Manduhai, *Tragic Spirits: Shamanism, Memory and Gender in Contemporary Mongolia* (Chicago, IL: University of Chicago Press, 2013)

Hoppál, Mihály, and Vilmos Diószegi (eds), *Folk Beliefs and Shamanistic Traditions in Siberia* (Budapest: Akadémiai Kiadó, 1996)

Mally, Stelmaszyk, *Shamanism in Siberia: Sound and Turbulence in Cursing Practices in Tuva* (Abingdon: Routledge, 2023)

Maskarinec, Gregory G., *The Rulings of the Night: An Ethnography of Nepalese Shaman Oral Texts* (Madison, WI: University of Wisconsin Press, 1995)

Nelson, Sarah M., *Shamanism and the Origin of States: Spirit, Power and Gender in East Asia* (Walnut Creek, CA: Left Coast Press, 2008)

Oppitz, Michael, *Shamans of the Blind Country: A Picture Book from the Himalaya* (Berlin: Galerie Buchholtz, 2021)

Peters, Larry, *Tibetan Shamanism: Ecstasy and Healing* (Berkeley, CA: North Atlantic Books, 2016)

Rozwadowski, Andrzej, and Maria M. Kośko (eds), *Spirits and Stones: Shamanism and Rock Art in Central Asia and Siberia* (Poznań: Eastern Studies Institute, Adam Mickiewicz University, 2002)

Sultanova, Razia, *From Shamanism to Sufism: Women, Islam and Culture in Central Asia* (London: I. B. Tauris, 2014)

Tae-gon, Kim, *The Paintings of Korean Shaman Gods: History, Relevance and Role as Religious Icons*, trans. Christina Han (Folkestone: Renaissance Book, 2018)

Ysslestine, J. Van, *Spirits from the Edge of the World: Classical Shamanism in Ulchi Society* (n.p.: Pathfinder Communications, 2018)

Yuguang, Fu (ed.), *Shamanic and Mythic Cultures of Ethnic Peoples in Northern China I: Shamanic Deities and Rituals* (Abingdon: Routledge, 2021)

Zarcone, Thierry, and Angela Hobart, *Shamanism and Islam: Sufism, Healing Rituals and Spirits in the Muslim Worlds* (London: I. B. Tauris, 2017)

AMERICAS

Bacigalupo, Ana Mariella, *Shamans of the Foye Tree: Gender, Power and Healing among the Chilean Mapuche* (Austin, TX: University of Texas Press, 2007)

Beyer, Stephan V., *Singing to the Plants: A Guide to Mestizo Shamanism in the Upper Amazon* (Albuquerque, NM: University of New Mexico Press, 2011)

Fausto, Carlos, *Warfare and Shamanism in Amazonia* (Cambridge: Cambridge University Press, 2012)

Hunt, Norman Bancroft, *Shamanism in North America* (Toronto: Key Porter Books, 2002)

Jilek, Wolfgang G., *Indian Healing: Shamanic Ceremonialism in the Pacific Northwest Today* (Surrey, BC: Hancock House, 1982)

Labate, Beatriz Caiuby, and Clancy Cavnar (eds), *Ayahuasca Shamanism in the Amazon and Beyond* (Oxford University Press, 2014)

Laugrand, Frederic, and Jarich G. Oosten, *Inuit Shamanism and Christianity: Transitions and Transformations in the Twentieth Century* (Montreal: McGill-Queen's University Press, 2010)

Lowell, John Bean, *California Indian Shamanism* (Ramona, CA: Ballena Press, 1992)

Pinkson, Tom Soloway, *Flowers of Wiricuta: A Gringo's Journey to Shamanic Power* (n.p.: Wakan Press, 1995); repr. as *The Shamanic Wisdom of the Huichol: Medicine Teachings for Modern Times* (Rochester, VT: Destiny Books, 2010)

Saladin d'Anglure, Bernard, *Inuit Stories of Being and Rebirth: Gender, Shamanism and the Third Sex* (Winnipeg: University of Manitoba Press, 2018)

VanPool, Christine, and Todd VanPool, *Signs of the Casas Grandes Shamans* (Salt Lake City, UT: University of Utah Press, 2007)

Wardwell, Allen, *Tangible Visions: Northwest Coast Indian Shamanism and its Art* (New York: Monacelli Press, 1996)

Whitley, David S., *The Art of the Shaman: Rock Art of California* (Salt Lake City, UT: University of Utah Press, 2000)

EUROPE

Ahlbäck, Tore, and Jan Bergman (eds), *The Saami Shaman Drum* (Turku: Donner Institute for Research in Religious and Cultural History, 1991)

Aldhouse-Green, Miranda, and Stephen Aldhouse-Green, *The Quest for the Shaman: Shape-Shifters, Sorcerers and Spirit Healers of Ancient Europe* (London: Thames & Hudson, 2005)

Blain, Jenny, *Nine Worlds of Seid-Magic: Ecstasy and Neo-Shamanism in North European Paganism* (London: Routledge, 2002)

Cowan, Tom, *Fire in the Head: Shamanism and the Celtic Spirit* (New York: HarperCollins, 1995)

Gardeła, Leszek, Sophie Bønding and Peter Pentz (eds), *The Norse Sorceress* (Oxford: Oxbow Books, 2023)

Ginzburg, Carlo, *Night Battles: Witchcraft and Agrarian Cults in the Sixteenth and Seventeenth Centuries*, trans. John and Anne Tedeschi (Baltimore, MD: John Hopkins University Press, 1983)

Hoppál, Mihály (ed.), *Shamanism in Eurasia* (Göttingen: Herodot, 1984)

AFRICA

Beattie, John, and John Middleton (eds), *Spirit Mediumship and Society in Africa* (London: Routledge, 2004)

Boddy, Janice, *Wombs and Alien Spirits: Women, Men and Zār Cult in Northern Sudan* (Madison, WI: University of Wisconsin Press, 1989)

Keney, Bradford P., *Bushman Shaman: Awakening the Spirit through Ecstatic Dance* (Rochester, VT: Destiny Books, 2005)

Lewis-Williams, David J., and Sam Challis, *Deciphering Ancient Minds: The Mystery of San Bushman Rock Art* (London: Thames & Hudson, 2011)

Lewis-Williams, David J., and Thomas Dowson, *Images of Power: Understanding Rock Art* (Johannesburg: Southern Book Publishers, 1999)

MODERN AND NEO-SHAMANISM

Artaud, Antonin, *Journey to Mexico: Revolutionary Messages and the Tarahumara*, trans. Rainer J. Hansche, ed. Stuart Kendell (New York: Contra Mundum, 2024)

Burroughs, William, and Allen Ginsberg, *The Yage Letters* (San Francisco, CA: City Light Books, 1963)

Castaneda, Carlos, *The Teachings of Don Juan: a Yaqui Way of Knowledge* (Berkeley, CA: University of California Press, 1968)

Firestone, Evan R., *Animism and Shamanism in Twentieth-Century Art: Kandinsky, Ernst, Pollock, Beuys* (London: Routledge, 2016)

Fonneland, Trude, *Contemporary Shamanism in Norway* (Oxford: Oxford University Press, 2017)

Harner, Michael, *The Way of the Shaman*, 3rd edn (New York: HarperCollins, 1990 [1980])

Huxley, Aldous, *The Doors of Perception* (Thinking Ink Media, 2011 [1957])

Kraft, Siv Ellen, Trude Fonneland and James R. Lewis (eds), *Nordic Neoshamanisms* (Houndmills: Palgrave Macmillan, 2015)

Noel, Daniel C., *The Soul of Shamanism* (New York: Continuum, 1997)

Wallis, Robert J., *Shamans/Neo-Shamans: Contested Ecstasies, Alternative Archaeologies and Contemporary Pagans* (London: Routledge, 2003)

Wasson, Gordon, *Soma: Divine Mushroom of Immortality* (New York: Harcourt Brace, 1968)

SOURCES OF ILLUSTRATIONS

Every effort has been made to locate and credit copyright holders of the material reproduced in this book. The author and publisher apologize for any omissions or errors, which can be corrected in future editions.

a = above, b = below, c = centre, l = left, r = right

1 Linden-Museum Stuttgart 2 Joseph Rock/GEO Image Collection/Bridgeman Images 3 Linden-Museum Stuttgart 4 The Metropolitan Museum of Art, New York. The Charles and Valerie Diker Collection of Native American Art, Gift of Valerie-Charles Diker Fund, 2017 6–7 National Museum of the American Indian, Smithsonian Institution (P33780) 8 © 1945, The Estate of Christoph von Fürer-Haimendorf. SOAS Library Special Collections reference PP MS 19/6/APA/0610 11 Christoph & Friends/Das Fotoarchiv/Alamy Stock Photo 12 Commissioned by Film London. Produced in association with Further up in the Air and Liverpool Housing Action Trust. Courtesy of Marcus Coates, and Kate MacGarry, London. Photo by Nick David 13l Smithsonian American Art Museum, Gift of Mrs Joseph Harrison, Jr, 1985.66.16 13r Hemis/Alamy Stock Photo 14 Kenneth Keifer/Alamy Stock Photo 15 Library of Congress, Washington, DC 16 Dmitriy Moroz/Alamy Stock Photo 17al The Trustees of the British Museum 17ac Wellcome Collection 17ar UtCon Collection/Alamy Stock Photo 17bl The Metropolitan Museum of Art, New York, The Charles and Valerie Diker Collection of Native American Art, Gift of Charles and Valerie Diker, 2019 17bc Art Images/Getty Images 17br The Natural History Museum/Alamy Stock Photo 18–19 Luisa Ricciarini/Bridgeman Images 20 NARA 21 Ernst Mankers, *Die lappische Zaubertrommel. Eine ethnologische Monographie*, 1938 22l The Trustees of the British Museum 22r Los Angeles County Museum of Art, Costume Council Fund (M.83.190.388) 23a Nicolaes Witsen, *Noord en Oost Tartarye...*, 1705 23bl Bibliothèque nationale de France 23br Reproduced by kind permission of the Syndics of Cambridge University Library 24 Hemis/Alamy Stock Photo 26l Georgiy Khoroshevskiy, 1931 26r Max Carocci, 2017 27l R. Gordon Wasson, *Soma: Divine Mushroom of Immortality*, 1972 27r William Burroughs and Allen Ginsberg, *The Yage Letters*, 1963 29 Maxim Sukharev 30 Still from *Shamans and the City* by Simona Piantieri, Simolab Creative AV 31 steeve-x-art/Alamy Stock Photo 33 Elisabeth Blanchet/Alamy Stock Photo 34–35 © Nanna Heitmann/Magnum Photos 36 Library of Congress, Washington, DC 38 Mark De Fraeye/akg-images 41 Feije Riemersma/Alamy Stock Photo 42l Steven Michaan Collection 42r Princeton University Art Museum. Lent by the Department of Geosciences, Princeton University 43l Los Angeles County Museum of Art, Gift of Constance McCormick Fearing (M.86.311.6) 43r Princeton University Art Museum, Princeton University Art Museum. Gift of Gillett G. Griffin 44 American Museum of Natural History Department of Anthropology 46 Mingei International Museum/Art Resource, New York 47al Los Angeles County Museum of Art, The Proctor Stafford Collection, purchased with funds provided by Mr and Mrs Allan C. Balch (M.86.296.154) 47ac Richard A. Cooke/Corbis/Getty Images 47ar Världskulturmuseet, Göteborg (Museum of World Culture) 1924.16.0038 47bl The Metropolitan Museum of Art, New York, Purchase, Oscar de la Renta Gift, 1997 47bc Granger – Historical Picture Archive/Alamy Stock Photo 47br Los Angeles County Museum of Art, Gift of Drs Alan Grinnell and Feelie Lee (M.2001.168.2) 48 Cavan Images/Alamy Stock Photo 49 Courtesy Michael Oppitz and Galerie Buchholz 50–51 Dagmar Hollmann 52l The Metropolitan Museum of Art, New York, The Charles and Valerie Diker Collection of Native American Art, Gift of Charles and Valerie Diker, 2021 52r The Metropolitan Museum of Art/Art Resource/Scala, Florence 53 B. Munkhbayar 54 Still from *Shamans and the City* by Simona Piantieri, Simolab Creative AV 55l Ulf Andersen/Getty Images 55r Pitt Rivers Museum/Bridgeman Images 57 imageBROKER.com GmbH & Co. KG/Alamy Stock Photo 58l Art Institute of Chicago, Gift of Ethel and Julian Goldsmith 58c Yale University Art Gallery, Gift of Mr and Mrs Fred Olsen 58r Museu de Arqueologia e Etnologia da Universidade de São Paulo 59a Jeff Foott/Nature Picture Library 59bl Owen Lattimore/Royal Geographical Society/Getty Images 59bc The Walters Art Museum, Gift of John G. Bourne, 2013 59br Boltin Picture Library/Bridgeman Images 60–61 © Claudia Andujar, courtesy Galeria Vermelho, São Paulo, Brazil 62 Transcendental Graphics/Getty Images 65 © A. Abbas/Magnum Photos 66–67 David Vilaplana/Alamy Stock Photo 68l Sipa US/Alamy Stock Photo 68r Quintana Galleries, Portland, Oregon. Photo Kevin McConnell Photography 69 Florencia Luna/AFP/Getty Images 70 The Metropolitan Museum of Art, New York, Gift of George D. Pratt, 1932 71al Afghanistan, Kaboul, Musée national © MNAAG, Paris, Dist. GrandPalaisRmn/Photo Thierry Ollivier 71ac The Trustees of the British

Museum **71ar** David Levenson/Alamy Stock Photo **71bl** The Metropolitan Museum of Art, New York. The Michael C. Rockefeller Memorial Collection, Bequest of Nelson A. Rockefeller, 1979 / the funkyfood London – Paul Williams/Alamy Stock Photo **71br** National Museum of the American Indian, Smithsonian Institution (22/8837). Photo by NMAI Photo Services **72** How Hwee Young/EPA/Shutterstock **73** REY Pictures/Alamy Stock Photo **74** Biodiversity Heritage Library **77** Transcendental Graphics/Getty Images **78** Jeon Heon-Kyun/EPA/Shutterstock **79** Courtesy of the Juan Negrín Family Archive **80** Ville Palonen/Alamy Stock Photo **81al** Mark De Fraeye/akg-images **81ac** Kevin Frayer/Getty Images **81ar** Ammit Jack/Shutterstock **81bl** Library of Congress, Washington, DC **81bc** Mark Eveleigh/Alamy Stock Photo **81br** Hemis/Alamy Stock Photo **83** Roberto Quijada **84–85** Images & Stories/Alamy Stock Photo **86** The Trustees of the British Museum **89** Sonoma County Library Photograph Collection **90** The Metropolitan Museum of Art, New York, Harris Brisbane Dick Fund, 1943 **91al** Peter & Dawn Cope Collection/Mary Evans Picture Library **91ac** World History Archive/Alamy Stock Photo **91ar, bl** Archives Charmet/Bridgeman Images **91bc** Album/Alamy Stock Photo **91br** steeve-x-art/Alamy Stock Photo **93** The Metropolitan Museum of Art, New York, Rogers Fund, 1917 **94** Tuul and Bruno Morandi/Alamy Stock Photo **95** © Makara Gallery. Jean-Jacques Lussier collection, Montreal. Photo Julien Hureau **96** The Picture Art Collection/Alamy Stock Photo **97** Diane Stoney/Alamy Stock Photo **98–99** The Picture Art Collection/Alamy Stock Photo **100l** Album/Alamy Stock Photo **100r** Paul Drozdowski **101l** Archives of The Grey Nuns of Montréal, private papers of Sister Pélagie Inuuk **101r** Esenia Sofronova **102** Miguel Vilca Vargas **105** Courtesy of the Royal Anthropological Institute **106–7** © Lu-Nan/Magnum Photos **108** Alpha Stock/Alamy Stock Photo **110** Luke Hancock **113** Library of Congress, Washington, DC **114** John Mitchell/Alamy Stock Photo **115** Dr Homayun Sidky **116–17** UCLA Latin American Institute **118** Courtesy Antony Galbraith **119l** Bob Daemmrich/Alamy Stock Photo **119r** Abbie Warnock-Matthews/Shutterstock **122** The Estate of Norval Morrisseau **123l** Art Institute of Chicago, African and Amerindian Art Purchase Fund **123r** Los Angeles County Museum of Art, Gift of Drs Alan Grinnell and Feelie Lee (M.2007.227.1) **124–25** The Cleveland Museum of Art, Gift of Mrs A. Dean Perry 1981.69 **126** The Trustees of the British Museum **127** The Metropolitan Museum of Art, New York. Bequest of Arthur M. Bullowa, 1993 **129** Werner Forman/Universal Images Group/Getty Images **130** © Claudia Andujar, courtesy Galeria Vermelho, São Paulo, Brazil **133** NPL – DeA Picture Library/Bridgeman Images **134** Russell Lee/NARA **135al** Luisa Ricciarini/Bridgeman Images **135ac** National Gallery of Art, Washington, Patrons' Permanent Fund **135ar** shflickinger/Shutterstock **135bl** Satoshi Takahashi/LightRocket/Getty Images **135bc** Sanjit Pariyar/NurPhoto/Getty Images **135br** Frantisek Staud/Alamy Stock Photo **136** Kjersti Joergensen **137l** Chronicle/Alamy Stock Photo **137r** Royal Geographical Society/Alamy Stock Photo **138** robert harding/Alamy Stock Photo **139** Roger Bamber/Alamy Stock Photo **141** © Raymond Depardon/Magnum Photos **142–43** Howard G. Charing and Peter Cloudsley, *The Ayahuasca Visions of Pablo Amaringo*, 2011 **144l** wittybear/123RF.com **144c** piemags/nature/Alamy Stock Photo **144r** Nancy Ayumi Kunihiro/Dreamstime.com **145al** ecuadorquerido/Adobe Stock **145ac** onapalmtree/Shutterstock **145ar** Reanne Crane/Shutterstock **145bl** dadalia/123RF.com **145bc** michael meijer/123RF.com **145br** grejak/123RF.com **146l** Khaled Desouki/AFP/Getty Images **146r** Eric Lafforgue. All rights reserved 2024/Bridgeman Images **147** Jacques Torregano/akg-images **148** Jacques Jangoux/Alamy Stock Photo **149al** Huy Hoan/Shutterstock **149ac** Orlando Barria/EPA-EFE/Shutterstock **149ar** Bjorn Svensson/Alamy Stock Photo **149bl** Heritage Image Partnership Ltd/Alamy Stock Photo **149bc** Gerhard Joren/LightRocket/Getty Images **149br** Monirul Bhuiyan/AFP/Getty Images **151** Franco Pinna, from the therapeutic dance cycle of Maria di Nardò (detail). Nardò (Salento, Italy), 1959 **152–53** Courtesy Anderson Debernardi **154** Wellcome Collection **157** Ladislaus Forbath, as related by Joseph Geleta, translated from the Hungarian by Lawrence Wolfe, *The New Mongolia* (London: William Heinemann Ltd, 1936) **158l** Courtesy of Waddington's Auctioneers and Appraisers, Toronto **158r** Steven Michaan Collection **159** Oyvind Martinsen Documentary Collection/Alamy Stock Photo **160** agf photo/Superstock **161** Sanavik Co-operative Ltd/Canadian Arctic Producers. Photo by RJ Ramrattan/Canadian Arctic Producers **162** Library of Congress, Washington, DC **163al** Photo Scala, Florence/bpk, Bildagentur für Kunst, Kultur und Geschichte, Berlin **163ac** Dallas Museum of Art, gift of Elizabeth H. Penn/Bridgeman Images **163ar** Tambaran Gallery, New York/Bridgeman Images **163bl** Werner Forman/Universal Images Group/Getty Images **163bc** The Metropolitan Museum of Art/Art Resource/Scala, Florence **163br** Universal History Archive/Universal Images Group/Getty Images **165** Library of Congress, Washington, DC **166** The Metropolitan Museum of Art, Gift of Roberta Lee Boxer, 1984 **167al** Dirk Bakker/Bridgeman Images **167ac** The Trustees of the British Museum **167ar** Museu de Arqueologia e Etnologia da Universidade de São Paulo **167bl** DeAgostini/Getty Images **167bc** The Metropolitan Museum of Art, New York, Gift of Albert J. Grant and Monique Grant Joint Revocable Trust, 2014 **167br** Los Angeles County Museum of Art, The Proctor Stafford Collection, purchased with funds provided by Mr and Mrs Allan C. Balch (M.86.296.55) **168l** robertharding/Alamy

Stock Photo 168r Leemage/Corbis/Getty Images 169l The Cleveland Museum of Art, Gift of the Hanna Fund 1957.24 169r The Trustees of the British Museum 170l Emilie Lesvignes 170c Heritage Image Partnership Ltd/Alamy Stock Photo 170r Pavel Filatov/Alamy Stock Photo 171a Chart based on schematic by J. D. Lewis-Williams and T. A. Dowson, published in *Current Anthropology*, Vol. 29, No. 2 (April 1988), p. 206 171bl Peregrine/Alamy Stock Photo 171bc Pulsar Imagens/Alamy Stock Photo 171br Porky Pies Photography/Alamy Stock Photo 172 The Trustees of the British Museum 173al American Museum of Natural History Department of Anthropology 173ac Granger – Historical Picture Archive/Alamy Stock Photo 173ar Världskulturmuseet, Göteborg (Museum of World Culture) 1880.04.0575 173bl Courtesy of the Indianapolis Museum of Art at Newfields, Gift of Mr and Mrs Eli Lilly 173bc Courtesy of Grusenmeyer Woliner Gallery, photo Studio Asselberghs, Frédéric Dehean 173br Världskulturmuseet, Göteborg (Museum of World Culture) 1892.03.0285 175 American Museum of Natural History Department of Anthropology 176 photo-fox/Alamy Stock Photo 178 Wellcome Collection 181 Marc Deville/Gamma-Rapho/Getty Images 182–83 Courtesy of the Natural History Museum of Los Angeles County 184 Mark De Fraeye/akg-images 185 Eric Baccega/Nature Picture Library 186 University of Michigan Library, Bentley Historical Library, Papa Isio (Oinosio Sigobela), HS4544 188l National Museum of the American Indian, Smithsonian Institution (15/9362) 188r Princeton University Art Museum. The Lloyd E. Cotsen, Class of 1950, Eskimo Bone and Ivory Carving Collection 1997–126 189 Hemis/Alamy Stock Photo 190–91 The Trustees of the British Museum 192 © A. Abbas/Magnum Photos 194l Werner Forman/Universal Images Group/Getty Images 194r John Zada/Alamy Stock Photo 195 Werner Forman/Universal Images Group/Getty Images 196, 197al © Dumbarton Oaks, Pre-Columbian Collection, Washington, DC 197ac Princeton University Art Museum, lent by the Department of Geosciences, Princeton University 197ar © Barbier-Mueller Collections, Dallas. Photo Studio Ferrazzini Bouchet 197bl American Museum of Natural History Department of Anthropology 197bc Museum of Fine Arts, Boston. All rights reserved/Gift of Landon T. Clay/Bridgeman Images 197br NSP-RF/Alamy Stock Photo 199 American Museum of Natural History Department of Anthropology 200 Sovfoto/Universal Images Group/Shutterstock 203 Pulsar Imagens 204 Museum of Archaeology and Anthropology, Cambridge 205al Roy Palmer/Shutterstock 205ac Dirk Bakker/Bridgeman Images 205ar The Metropolitan Museum of Art, New York. The Michael C. Rockefeller Memorial Collection, Bequest of Nelson A. Rockefeller, 1979 205bl The Trustees of the British Museum 205bc The Cleveland Museum of Art, Gift of Mrs R. Henry Norweb, Mrs Albert S. Ingalls, with additions from the John L. Severance Fund 1952.459 205br © musée du quai Branly – Jacques Chirac, Dist. GrandPalaisRmn/Photo Patrick Gries/Benoit Jeanneton 206 © musée du quai Branly – Jacques Chirac, Dist. GrandPalaisRmn/Photo Michel Urtado/Thierry Ollivier 207 Sipa US/Alamy Stock Photo 208–9 National Museum of Korea (Bongwan14319) 210 Dreamstime.com 212 Världskulturmuseet, Göteborg (Museum of World Culture) 1892.03.0354 214l © LDA Saxony-Anhalt, Karol Schauer 214r © LDA Sachsen-Anhalt, Andrea Hörentrup 215 Mark Fox/Alamy Stock Photo 216 François Guénet/akg-images 217l Rijksmuseum, Amsterdam 217r Rabatti & Domingie/akg-images 218 The Trustees of the British Museum 219al The Cleveland Museum of Art, Gift of Brian and Florence Mahony 1995.244 219ac National Museum of Denmark Photo Arnold Mikkelsen 219ar porpeller/123RF 219bl © musée du quai Branly – Jacques Chirac, Dist. GrandPalaisRmn/Photo Claude Germain 219bc Fenimore Art Museum, Cooperstown, New York, Loan from the Eugene V. and Clare E. Thaw Charitable Trust, Thaw Collection, T0214. Photo John Bigelow Taylor, New York 219br ArtBlackburn, Marfa, Texas 220al, cl McCord Stewart Museum Montreal, Gift of Dr George Mercer Dawson 220bl CM Dixon/Heritage Images/Getty Images 220br Världskulturmuseet, Göteborg (Museum of World Culture), 1925.12.0002 221 The Walters Art Museum, Gift of John Bourne, 2009 223 Andrea Robinson/Getty Images 224 Sally Anderson/Alamy Stock Photo 227 Rudi Sebastian/Alamy Stock Photo 228 Northern Exposure by JR/Shutterstock 229 AfriPics.com/Alamy Stock Photo 230l Bob Daemmrich/Alamy Stock Photo 230r NSP-RF/Alamy Stock Photo 231al Elena Odareeva/Dreamstime.com 231ar Sailingstone Travel/Alamy Stock Photo 231bl Sergei Konstantinov/Dreamstime.com 231br Nikolay Mihalchenko/Alamy Stock Photo 232 Neil Bowman/Alamy Stock Photo 233 Gianni Dagli Orti/Shutterstock 234l Insights/Universal Images Group/Getty Images 234r DEA/G. Dagli Orti/De Agostini/Getty Images 235 Feng Qu 236 Jan Butchofsky/Alamy Stock Photo 237al Elena Nazarova/Dreamstime.com 237ac Bayar Balgantseren/imageBROKER/Shutterstock 237ar Panther Media GmbH/Alamy Stock Photo 237bl Corentin Le Gall/Alamy Stock Photo 237bc, br Daan Kloeg/Shutterstock 238 *The Popular Science Monthly*, June 1898 239 mehmetozb/123RF.com 241 Deana Paqua, embodythesacred.net. Featuring *Andean Energy Healing Cards* by Eileen O'Hare and *Faery Blessing Cards* by Lucy Cavendish 243 Jorge Mañes Rubio, from the *On Distant Objects And Hungry Gods* series, 2017. Courtesy the artist 244–45 Hemis/Alamy Stock Photo

INDEX

Illustrations are in **bold**.

Abramović, Marina 10
Achuar shamans 69, **215**
activism 82
Afghanistan 71, 99, 208
agency, animism 49–52
Aguada culture 71
Alaska *see also* Inuit people
  Christianity 100, 103
  Haida culture 62, **76**, 77, **126**, **197**, 211, **220**
  maskettes **176**
  Punuk culture **188**
  Tlingit culture 42, 87, 124–25, **158**, **165**, **197**, **219**, 238
  Yup'ik shamans **4**, 46, 52, **163**
Aleutian Islands 103
Alevi-Bektashi 98
Algonquian people 226–28
altars 240, **241**, **242**, **243**
Amanita muscaria **145**
Amazon 26, 56, 72, **149**, **215** *see also* Brazil; Colombia; Ecuador; Peru
amulets **42**–43, 58, 76, **168**, 172–73, **217**
ancestors 42, 52, 64, **95**, 118, 121, 190
androgyny 188
animals
  depiction of 58–59, **168**
  doubles 47, 222
  masters and mistresses of 69, **70**–71, 104, 118–19, 140
  perspectivism 45–49
  profiles 58–59
  sacrifices 81
  shape-shifting **194**, 196–97
animism
  agency 49–52
  dualism 56
  growth and revival in 21st century 55–56
  personhood 54–55
  perspectivism 45–49, 56
  use of term 40–42

Anishinaabe people 74, 122, 228
anthropomorphism 17, 47, **116**–17, **123**, **164**, **168**, **173**, 196–97, **213**, 236–37
Apatani people 8, 211
apprentices 73, 198
Arawakan people **144**, 226, 228, 238–39
archetypes 90–91
Argentina 71
art *see also* paintings
  modern shamanism 10
  motifs 122–23, **124**–25, **126**, 127–28, **169**, 170–71, **182**, 206, 211
  perception 123, **125**
  role of, and concepts 202
ASC (Alternative (or Adjusted) State of Consciousness)
  behaviours 134–35, 136–40, 146–50, 184
  clothing 198, 214
  definition of 132
  entoptic phenomena 169
  music 215–16
  non-shamans 13, 25
  psychotropics 140, 233
  rock art depictions 128
Asia, Central 12, **59**, 99, 236–37 *see also specific countries*
Asia, South East 52 *see also specific countries*
axis mundi 48, 166–67, 211
ayahuasca 140, **142**–43, **145**, 152–53
Aztecs 205

babaylan **186**, 187
ballcourts 121
bears 59
Bektashi order 132
bells **213**
benandanti 101, **149**
bi **173**
bindings used in ceremonies 75, **195**
birds 58, 96, 121, 160, **173**, **197**, 207
black magic 20
blacksmiths 72–73
blades **192**, **193**

Blue Pearl Ice Festival 53
bodies
  differences and shamans 184–85
  impermeability to wounds 75, **193**, 195
body paint, Yanomami 48
Bole Maru cult 89
Bolivia **66**–67
Bön 88, 95, 97
Brazil
  Santarém 47, **164**, **167**, 168
  vessels 218
  Wauja people **203**
Bronson, AA 10
Buddhism 88, 96–97, 106–7, 140
  Tibetan Buddhism **95**, 97, 106–7, **149**
burials 47, 121, **126**, 164, 165, 214, **231**, 238, **239**
Burroughs, William 27
Buryat shamans 23, 72–73, 83, 185, **216**, 231
Bwiti cults 20

cairns *see* ovoo
Canada *see* North America
candles 240, **241**
cannabis 221 *see also* hemp
Caribbean 103, 113, **219**
caryatids 47
Casas Grandes jar **182**–83
Castaneda, Carlos 27
Çatalhöyük, Turkey 71
cave paintings *see* rock art
caves 14, 121, 137, 230, 232, 233
charms 172–73, 240, **241**
Chavín de Huántar, Peru 234
Chibcha 168, 205
China
  bi **173**
  Communism 25–26
  Daur people 235
  divination 72
  gender 188–89
  Liangzhu culture 207
  Nanai shamans **175**
  Naxi shamans 2
  organized religion positions 21

  robes 92–96
  shaman iconography 92
  shrines **244**–45
  spirit guardians **164**
Chocó shamans 188
Christianity 45, 88–89, 100–105, 112, **113**, 132, 133, 135, 137, 150–51, 162, 240 *see also* Native American Church
cleansing ceremonies 69
clothing 76, 92–96, 175, 187, 202–6, 207, 210, 211, **212**–13, 214
Coates, Marcus 10, **12**
coca 166, **169**, 228
Coclé culture **123**
cohoba **144**, 167
Colombia 71, **116**–17, **164**, 166, 167, 168, **197**, 232
colonialism 103
communication technologies, non-written 202
cong 207
copper 205
Core Shamanism 30–31, 216, 240–41
cosmic pillar/tree 48, **49**, 120–21, 168–69, **175**, 208, 211
cosmos *see also* reality
  animism 40, 45–48, 56
  axis mundi 48, 166–67, 211
  dualism 56
  personhood 53–54
  Taíno people 120–21
Costa Rica 58, 71, **197**, 205, 221
counterculture 27–28
Cree First Nations 75
crocodiles 58, **166**
crystals 205, 240, **241**
Cuba **147**
cultural heritage 28
Cuna shamans 111
Czech Republic 17

dance 92, **93**, 96, 98, 147, 151
'das log 97
datura 86, 92, **145**
Daur people 235
death ceremonies **65**, 126, **194**, 238

decolonization 27, 174
deer 17, 58, 208, 237
deer stones 236-37
demons 118
dervish dancers 93
dhyāngro 94-95
dimensions 156-59, 174, 187, 226, 228-29
distaffs 219
divination 25, 72, 74, 92, 96, **149**, 198, 211, 234, 240
Dixon, Roland 15
Dorset culture 47
doubles 222
Dowson, Thomas A. 170
dreams 118, 119, 128, 149, 160
drums 30, **44**, 72, **94-95**, 97, 101, **105**, 138-39, **146**, 200, 213, 215, 216-20, 223
dualism 163
dukun 73
duty 64

ecology 55
ecstasy 132, 135, 137
Ecuador 69, 140, 215
effigies 173, 190-91, 206, 213
Eliade, Mircea 27, 55, 146
Embera shaman 159
emetics 219
entheogens 127 *see also* psychotropics
entoptic phenomena 169, 170-71
ergi 32
Evenk people 164, 173, 205, 211
exorcisms 15

faces 18-19, 125, 161, 237, 163
feathers 6-7, 22, 34-35, 46, 162-63, 176, 200, 207, 223
Fingo witch doctor 23
Finland 25, 229
Finno-Ugrian animism 32, 82
flesh offerings 81
flight, harpoon counterweights 17
flying 127, 128, 207

food offerings 81
forces, invisible 156-59
France 17, 170, 189
fringes 11, 13, 23, 53, 178, 200, 206, 207, 212, 213, 214, 216, 224
frogs 58, 167, 168, 222

Gabon 20
Gabyshev, Alexander 101
gender 180, 185-88
Germany 91, 214
ghosts 69, 238
Ginsberg, Allen 27
gold 205, 208-9
graves 164, **165**, 214, 238
Greenland 194
greenstones 205
grindstones 221, 222
Gundestrup cauldron 71

Haida culture 62, 76, 77, 126, **197**, 211, 220
Haiti 149
hallucinations 138
hallucinogens *see* psychotropics
Harner, Michael 30, 216
harpoon counterweights 17
headdresses 17, 18-19, 76, 207, **208-9**, 211-14, 233
healing ceremonies
  common elements 76
  drums 139
  Haida shamans 76, 77
  Hmong shamans 68
  holistic and spiritual approach 68-69
  Huichol people 13
  Indonesia 73
  Malaysia 138
  Mongolia 11
  music 99
  negative forces 20-21
  Nepal 115
  potions 91
  trance 150
  witch doctors 20
  X-ray vision 127
  helpers **44**, 66, 158, 160-61, 164, 165, 168, 213
hemp 145 *see also* cannabis
hereditary shamans 78-79

hermits 137
Herodotus 15
hierarchy, lack of 75-78
Himalayan region
  Apatani people 8, 211
  Idu Mishmi people 210, 211, 238
  shamans 24, 106-7
Hinduism 86, 88, 92, 132, **136**
Historia Norwegie 9, 15
history, shamanism in antiquity 16-19
Hmong shamans 68
horses 41, **59**, 99, 237
Horwitz, Jonathan 216
Huichol people 13, 81, 104, **114**, 122, 231, 234
Hungary 25, 32, **98-99**, 100
hysteria 137-38, 184

Iban shamans 193-94
idol, Shigir 17
Idu Mishmi people 210, 211, 238
illness *see also* healing ceremonies
  as living entity 39
  spiritual sources 115, 156
  theft of soul 21, 69
incantation 91
incense 81
incorporeality 156, 161
India *see also* Hinduism
  link to past 26-27
Indonesia 73, 187, 193-94
Indus Valley 18-19
initiation rituals 161-64
inner vision 198, **199**
instruments 218-19, 221-22
intangibility 45, 112-15, 126, 156
intercessions 69
international events 82, 83
Inuit people 20-21, 101, 118, 119, 140, 158, 161-63, 173, 195, 211
Iran 70
iron 205
Islam 88, **93**, 98, 99, 132
Isogaisa Festival 33
Italy 101, 147, 151

jade 173, 205, 208-9
jaguars **48**, 52, 56, 59, 196-97, 234
jaibaná 188
jhākris 94

Kashaya Pomo people 89
Kazakhstan 215, 231, 239
Kholmatov, Tasmat 187
Khorezm 187
Kichwa shamans 140
kobyz 98-99, 215
Komi people 100
Korea
  ancestors 64
  blades **192**, 193
  death ceremonies 65
  initiation rituals 78
  landscape 228
  mansin 242
  mudang 96, **184**, 192
  organized religion
  positions 21, 96
  paintings 38
  public ceremonies 243
  Silla crown 208-9
Kumandin shamans 63
Kwakwaka'wakw
  transformation masks 47

landscape, sacredness 226-29, 230-31, 232-42
Lewis, Ioan 20
Lewis-Williams, David 169, 170
Liangzhu culture 207
libations 66, 69, 81
Lion-person 50-51

machi 154
Malaysia 26, **138**, 160, 187
Mansi people 226
mansin 242
Mapuche 104, **154**, 187, 215, 219
marketing 28
masks
  artefacts in museums 222
  Haida shamans 77
  healing ceremonies 76
  helpers 164
  Inuit people 161-63, 239
  Kwakwaka'wakw 47

Nuxalk First Nations 1, 3
Olmecs 43
Pazyryk 59
Tlingit culture 219
Wauja people 203
X-ray vision 129
Yup'ik 4, 46, 52
medicine men 13 *see also* witch doctors
meditation 128, 135, 140, 226
mesa altars 240, 241
mescal 104, 144
mestizo shamans 140
metals 204-5, 213
Mexico
 European depictions 22
 Huichol people 13, 81, 104, 114, 122, 231, 234
 Mogollon culture 182-83
 Nayarit figurines 58, 167
 Olmecs 43, 196-97
 religious integration of shamans 24-25
 rock art 233
 syncretism 104
milk sprinkling 40, 41, 84-85
Milky Way 238
minerals 204-5
mirrors 211, 237
Mogollon culture 182-83
Mongolia
 Buryat shamans 216
 clothing 206
 effigies 164
 healing ceremonies 11
 invisible forces 157
 milk sprinkling 40, 41
 monuments 224
 organized religion positions 21
 ovoo 80, 235
 prohibitions 76
 rituals 53, 72
 sky 52, 235
 Tengrism 52, 96-97, 235
mudang 96, 184, 192
multiverse 45-48
Murugan 132, 136
mushrooms 27, 145, 168, 221
music 76, 91, 98-99, 146, 214-15 *see also* drums
myth 90-91

n/om 149
Nanabozho 226-28
Nanai people 36, 168, 175, 228
Native American Church 104, 145
nativism 32, 82, 89, 222
nats 181
Naxi shamans 2
near-death experiences 91, 128
Nechung oracle 149
Neo-Paganism 32, 214
Neo-Shamanism 31-32, 139, 174, 214, 216
neocolonialism 28-30
Nepal 49, 94-95, 115, 223
netherworld *see* underworld
New Age spirituality 30-31, 139
noaidi 101
non-binarism 185-87
North America *see also* Alaska; Mexico
 Algonquian people 226-8
 animals 59
 Anishinaabe people 74, 122, 228
 caves 14, 230
 Christianity 103-4
 European depictions of 22
 masks 1, 3
 medicine men 13
 mirrors 211
 Salish people 103, 105
 self-sacrifice 81
 shaking tents 74, 75
 sucking tubes 220
 Timucua diviners 15
 Nuxalk First Nations 1, 3

obsidian 205
offerings 40, 41, 66, 80-81, 80, 235
Ojibwa First Nations 75
Old Norse 32
Olmecs 43, 196-97
opium 144
Orochen shamans 204
other-than-human beings 53-54, 115, 188
ovoo 80, 235

paintings *see also* rock art
 Korea 38
Palmer, Craig 20
Panama 47, 111, 123, 159, 168, 169
Paracas culture 127
paraphernalia 202, 206-7, 210, 218-19
Parrish, Essie 89
Pashupati seal 18-19
Pazyryk horse mask 59
Pelagie Inuk 101
personhood 53-54
perspectivism 45, 46-47, 49, 56
Peru
 Arawakan people 226, 228, 238-39
 ayahuasca 140, 142-43, 145
 Chavín de Huántar 234
 landscape 228
 Paracas culture 127
 Q'eros 240-41
 religious integration of shamans 24-25
 Shipibo-Conibo 54, 64, 102, 110
 Tenon heads 234
petroglyphs *see* rock art
Petrov, Avvakum 15
peyote 6-7, 81, 104, 145
phalluses 18-19, 189
Philippines 186, 187
Piantieri, Simona 30, 54
piercing 81, 92, 132, 136, 193
place, sacredness 226-29, 230-31, 232-42
plants 142-45, 159, 161, 168, 169, 221-22
Ponce monolith 66-67
portals 116, 162, 173, 228-29, 239
possession 135, 140, 147, 150
potions 91
prayers 81
Primitive Religion (Tylor) 40
prohibitions 76, 103, 162
psychopomps 14, 91, 194, 238
psychotropics 25, 27, 58, 66, 91-92, 128, 130, 144-45, 189, 211, 218, 233-34
public ceremonies 73-75, 82
pulingaws 193
Punuk culture 188

Q'eros 240-41
quartz 205
quests 91

rapture 132, 135
rattles 68, 219
reality
 dimensions 156-59, 174, 187, 226
 intangibility 45, 112-15, 126, 156
 visions 118-22
reincarnation 49, 126
religion *see also* syncretism
 animism 42-43
 integration of shamans 21-25, 96
 syncretism 88
 visions 132
remote viewing 159
resurrection 91
rituals
 elements in cosmos 78
 range and common elements 79-82
rnga 97
Robber's Roost 14
robes 92-96, 175
rock art 12, 17, 59, 108, 119, 127-28, 169, 170-71, 189, 197, 211, 229, 230-31, 232-33
Rodnovery 82
Russia
 burials 231
 Buryat shamans 23, 72-73, 83, 185, 231
 censorship 101
 Nanai shamans 175
 revival of shamanism 26, 34-35
 Slavic healers 29, 31
 Soviet propaganda 26
 Tungus shamans 199
 Tuvan shamans 34-35, 84-85, 200, 207

Saami 15, 21, 33, 72, 100–101, 217
sacrifices 80–81, 237
St Peter the Aleut 100
St Stephen of Perm 100
St Teresa of Avila 132, 133
Salish people 103, 105
San Agustín culture 164
San Pedro cactus 145, 234
San people 149, 170–71, 197, 229
sangoma 24–25, 186
Sanskrit 14
Santarém 47, 164, 167, 168
Santeria 147
Scandinavia 174
    Gundestrup cauldron 71
    Neo-Paganism 32
    Saami 15, 21, 33, 72, 100–101, 217
science 112, 123–26
Scythians 221, 237
seances 106–7, 140–47, 150, 158–60, 184
second sight 126–27, 195–98
Sedna 118, 119
self-sacrifice 81
Selkup people 211
Serbia 17
sexuality 18, 189, 193
shadows 156
shaking tents 74, 75
shamanic journeys 135, 139, 140, 159–60, 239
shamans
    apprentices 73
    calling 79, 161, 180, 184
    European depictions of 22–23, 90–91
    first use of term 15
    growth and revival in 21st century 25, 26–27, 55–56, 82
    key concepts 12–14
    linguistic roots 12, 14
    syncretic 55
    use of term 10–12, 20, 25
Shamans and the City (Piantieri) 30, 54
shape-shifting 17, 66, 91, 122, 163, 166, 193–94 *see also* transformation
Shigir idol 17

Shipibo-Conibo 54, 64, 102, 110
Shiva 18, 86, 92, 95
shrines 235, 240, 241, 242, 244–45
Siberia
    amulets and effigies 173
    animals 59
    Buryat shamans 72–73
    Chukchi 187
    clothing 187, 207, 211, 212–13, 214
    cosmic tree 168–69
    European depictions of 22, 23
    Evenk people 164, 173, 205, 211
    iron 205
    Mansi people 226
    Nanai people 36, 175, 228
    seances 140
    Selkup people 211
    shamanism origins 12, 14, 15, 20
    Stephen of Perm 100
    Tungus shamans 44, 178
    Yakut shamans 239
Silla crown 208–9
simultaneity 125
Siona shamans 57
Sioux nations 75
sky 52, 53, 121, 235
Slavic healers 29, 31
Slavic Native Faith (Rodnovery) 31, 32, 82
smoke 81, 220, 239
snuff 66, 220, 221
soma 91, 92
Soma (Wasson) 27
sorcerers 118
soul catchers 220
souls
    Christian usage of term 45
    illnesses 21, 69
    number 156
    projection 193
South Africa 24–25, 171, 197, 229, 230
South America 28, 52, 190
spirit guardians 164
spirit guides 160, 161, 164
spirit helpers 18, 92, 160–61, 164, 168

spirit journeys 13, 104, 120–21, 149
spirits
    ancestors 52
    communication ceremonies 75
    possession 135, 140, 147, 150
staffs 29, 219, 222
Star Carr, UK 17
Steadman, Lyle 20
stools 58, 71, 166–67, 190, 211, 222
subterranean realms *see* underworld
sucking tubes 20, 76, 220
Sufism 93, 98, 99, 132, 137
summoning, paintings 38
Swanton, John Reed 15
syncretism 88, 104, 174

Taíno people 47, 120–21, 144, 167, 190–91, 219
Tairona shamanism 197
Taiwan 193
táltos 98–99, 100
Tamang people 94–95
tarantate 147–50, 151
Tarot cards 240, 241
tattoos 237
tears 66
teleportation 128, 135 *see also* shamanic journeys
Tengrism 52, 88, 96, 235
tents 74, 75, 239, 242
textiles 110, 119, 122, 124–25, 127, 240, 241
Tibetan Buddhism 95, 97, 106–7, 149
tigers 18–19, 92
Timucua diviners 15
Tiwanaku culture 66–67
Tlingit culture 42, 87, 124–25, 158, 165, 197, 219, 238
tobacco 59, 116, 144, 182–83, 220
tonal 47
tourism 26, 28
trance 13, 24, 73, 92, 128, 132, 135, 137, 138, 146–47, 216 *see also* ASC
transformation 17, 52, 66, 91, 188, 196–97, 234 *see also* shape-shifting
transgenderism 189–93
transvestism 188

tripartite face 18–19
Tukano people 116–17
Tungus shamans 44, 178, 199
tupilaq 194
Turanism 32
Turkey 71, 98–99
Tuvan shamans 34–35, 84–85, 200, 207
Tylor, Edward Burnett 40, 42, 45, 55

underworld 21, 63, 68–69, 91, 97, 121, 126
Ural mountains 17
urban animism 55–56
Uzbekistan 99, 187

Vietnam 149
vilca seeds 66
visions 21, 113, 114, 116–17, 118–22, 132, 152–53, 174
Vodou 149
volkhvs 29, 31, 82
völvas 32, 72

wands 219
Wasson, R. Gordon 27
Wauja people 203
The Way of the Shaman (Harner) 30
weapons 76, 237
witch doctors 20, 23 *see also* medicine men
witchcraft 62
Witsen, Nicolaes 15

X-ray vision 127, 129
Xa, Zadie 10

The Yage Letters (Burroughs & Ginsberg) 27
yãkoana 130
Yakut shamans 239
Yanomami people 48, 60–61, 141
yoga 18–19
yogis 132, 140
Yuman tribes 234
Yup'ik shamans 4, 46, 52, 163

Zãr cult 15, 146, 147
zemis 190–91
Zoroastrianism 88, 91, 92

255   INDEX

ACKNOWLEDGMENTS

My most sincere thanks go to the team at Thames & Hudson for assisting with the editing, production and design of the book. My acknowledgments go to Jane Laing, Florence Allard, Agatha Smith, Sadie Butler, Jo Walton, Carolyn Jones and Francesca Anderson.

Grateful thanks go to Robert J. Wallis, Martin Schulz and Simona Piantieri, whose generosity, intellectual stimulation and enthusiasm permeate this book.

Further thanks go to Marcus Coates, Jorge Mañes Rubio, Michael Oppitz, Paul Drozdowski, Miguel Vilca Vargas, Deana Paqua, Antony Galbraith and Maxim Sukharev, who gracefully allowed us to use their artworks and photographs.

Finally, I'd like to wholeheartedly thank my partner, Gihan Kanishka Pilana Withanage, whose loving encouragement supported me throughout the process.

ABOUT THE AUTHOR

Max Carocci is a socio-cultural anthropologist and is currently associate professor in Art History and Visual Cultures at the American University in London. For twelve years, he designed and taught the World Arts programme for Birkbeck College, London, in partnership with the British Museum. As well as having published numerous articles for scholarly and popular publications, he is the co-editor of *Art, Shamanism and Animism* (2022) and *Art, Observation and an Anthropology of Illustration* (2022). He has curated numerous exhibitions and worked as anthropological consultant for institutions such as the British Museum, the Royal Academy of Arts and the Horniman Museum in London, UK, the Weltkulturen Museum in Frankfurt, Germany, and the Musée du Nouveau Monde in La Rochelle, France, among others.

Front cover **Alutiiq mask, Kodiak Island, Alaska, 19th century**
Acquired by the ethnographer Alphonse Pinart during his voyage to Alaska in 1871–72, this mask is testimony to the rich shamanic cultures that pre-date Christian conversion. Sugpiaq Photo Benoît Touchard/© GrandPalaisRmn.

Back cover **A shaman prays during a summer solstice ritual, Ulaanbaatar, Mongolia, 2018**
Gestures such as the one shown in this image epitomize the importance of the inner sight sought - and achieved - by shamans in their rites and ceremonies. Kevin Frayer/Getty Images.

Pages 1 & 3 **Eagle transformation mask, British Columbia, Canada, 19th century**
Through ropes and folds, this Nuxalk mask can open and close, revealing an inner and outer face. Objects such as this remind us that beings can transform into one another at will. This is a central concept in shamanism as shamans can shape-shift or enter the body of another being to see through their eyes.

Page 2 **Joseph Rock, Naxi shaman, Yunnan, China, 1920s**
Naxi shamanism has been influenced by Tibetan Buddhism.

Page 4 **Yup'ik shamanic mask, Alaska, c. 1900**
The beings represented on this and similar masks convey the concept of transformation that is central to Arctic shamanism.

Pages 6–7 **Vita Rose, peyote ceremony, 1996–99**
As a plant that is used in ceremonies, peyote is central to modern Native American religions, such as the Native American Church.

First published in the United Kingdom in 2025 by Thames & Hudson Ltd, 6–24 Britannia Street, London WC1X 9JD

First published in the United States of America in 2025 by Thames & Hudson Inc., 500 Fifth Avenue, New York, New York, 10110

Shamans © 2025 Thames & Hudson Ltd, London

Text © 2025 Max Carocci

For image copyright information, see pages 249–251

All Rights Reserved. No part of this publication may be reproduced or transmitted in any form or by any means, electronic or mechanical, including photocopy, recording or any other information storage and retrieval system, without prior permission in writing from the publisher.

EU Authorized Representative:
Interart S.A.R.L.
19 rue Charles Auray, 93500 Pantin, Paris, France
productsafety@thamesandhudson.co.uk
interart.fr

A CIP catalogue record for this book is available from the British Library

Library of Congress Control Number 2025934800

ISBN 978-0-500-02868-1
01

Printed and bound in China by C&C Offset Printing Co. Ltd

Be the first to know about our new releases, exclusive content and author events by visiting
thamesandhudson.com
thamesandhudsonusa.com
thamesandhudson.com.au